65

NO EASY ANSWERS

ALSO BY ENOCH POWELL

The Rendel Harris Papyri 1936
First Poems 1937
A Lexicon to Herodotus 1938
The History of Herodotus 1939
Casting-off, and other poems 1939
Herodotus, Book VIII 1939
Llyfr Blegywryd (with Stephen Williams) 1942
Thucydidis Historia 1942
Herodotus (translation) 1949
Dancer's End and The Wedding Gift (poems) 1951
The Social Services: Needs and Means 1952
One Nation (jointly) 1950
Change is Our Ally (jointly) 1954
Biography of a Nation (with Angus Maude) 1955
Great Parliamentary Occasions 1960
Saving in a Free Society 1960
A Nation not Afraid 1965
Medicine and Politics 1966
The House of Lords in the Middle Ages (with Keith Wallis) 1968
Freedom and Reality 1969
The Common Market: the Case Against 1971
Still to Decide 1972

NO EASY ANSWERS

Enoch Powell

SHELDON PRESS
LONDON

First published in Great Britain in 1973 by
Sheldon Press, Marylebone Road, London NW1 4DU

Printed in Great Britain by
Northumberland Press Limited
Gateshead

ISBN 0 85969 001 6

CONTENTS

ACKNOWLEDGEMENTS

The author and publishers wish to acknowledge their thanks to Douglas Brown, Trevor Huddleston, Joseph McCulloch, Malcolm Muggeridge and Professor Dennis Nineham for permission to use their respective dialogues and to Mr Duffield, Editor of *News Extra* for permission to reproduce *That Cup of Cold Water*.

INTRODUCTION

I am glad that the Sheldon Press should feel that the pieces in this book may have a use and value slightly less ephemeral than the occasions for which they were written originally. Those occasions, which were nearly all unsought by the speaker (or writer), extend over fifteen years of my life. They were years during which, in part consciously, but probably even more below the conscious surface of the mind, I was almost continuously reflecting on certain words and passages and ideas; and it has seemed to me that, if I have not been going forward in comprehension of them, at least I have been going deeper. The reader will, for instance, occasionally notice that a text, such as 'the things that are Caesar's' (Matt. 22.21; Mark 12.17), has yielded a different result at different times and levels.

We are all prisoners of our personalities; and I fear it will be all too evident that for me intellectual effort—the grinding, polishing, drilling activity of the mind—is an inescapable and large ingredient in religion, as in so many of the other good things of life. Often when in church I have the guilty sense of playing truant by thinking when I ought to be praying. My excuse, like Boswell's for being a Scotsman, is the weak one that 'I cannot help it'; or perhaps I ought to say, that I have, as yet, learnt no better. At all events, many such a moment, sometimes in a service which has otherwise been a failure—and no two are alike, or equally successful or unsuccessful—has set me on a mental quest at the end of which I seemed to find something over which others too might 'rejoice with me' (Luke 15.9).

But how did I come to be there at all?

The biographical facts can be briefly told. My mother, whose knowledge of the Bible was phenomenal, had got her Christianity the hard way, and lost it again the hard way. She insisted—though insistence was not necessary—that I should know the Bible and know the Prayer Book and be confirmed in the Church of England. 'One day', she used to say, 'you may want to find what I no longer possess. Then it will be there waiting for you. I shall have done what I could.' It so happened that she also gave me the other key; for she taught me my first Greek, and indeed I still have the Greek Testament in which, as a girl learning Greek by herself, she followed the lessons in Newport, Salop, parish church.

A school with a strong divinity and Hellenistic tradition encouraged me to read the Greek Testament with more than a cursory eye to the commentaries and the textual criticism; and in the process I discovered that the Gospel was 'not true'. The historical and internal evidence would not support the narrative. The textual evidence pointed only too clearly to the sort of process by which that narrative had been evolved. Worse still, the features of the narrative were not unique: they were documented over and over again from the most primitive cultures to the most advanced; and the central feature of the drama, the incarnate god who is killed and eaten, was widespread almost to the point of universality. Worst of all, religion itself, and not only Christianity, could be accounted for as a device for meeting certain psychological needs or cravings; but these surely could and should be overcome in other ways? Between them, textual criticism, history and the psychology of religion had made, as Nietzsche put it, 'a clean sweep' (*reinen Tisch*).

There is a certain temperament to which falsehood, and particularly institutionalized falsehood, cannot be a matter of indifference, and to which agnosticism appears only a lazier form of superstition: Saul of Tarsus was no agnostic. Once gained, an insight must be communicated. It is intolerable not merely to be a lip-server of error, but to be a passive observer of it. For twenty years I lived and practised and, as opportunity offered, propagated the negative consequences of what my training and education had made clear to me beyond all possibility of refutation: it would need more than a miracle to overturn the logic of history, comparative religion, anthropology and psychology. The news that 'God is dead' did not depend on hearsay: the process was irreversible.

Actually, as I now perceive in retrospect, the atheism had become a dogma, a closed and fixed conclusion, and my mind and attention had moved elsewhere. Perhaps it is part of the story that for seven years they were concentrated as near as may be exclusively upon war. Wartime was for part of the mind an intellectual hibernation—all the more profound because of the intensity of the application to the mechanics of military victory. The war, too, once it was over, relegated all that had gone before it to the status of a closed epoch, a book which had been sealed.

One winter Sunday not long after the war I did something against my will and against my better judgement. I entered a church just before evensong and sat down. For twenty years I had never crossed the threshold of any church except for architectural curiosity, and that rarely. I felt ashamed of what I was doing, because I could not give myself a satisfactory account for it. So I chose a dark corner, near the door, hoping to escape my own notice. However, ashamed or not, I came again and again, until presently I realized that I was caught fast, not by anything external, whether personal or material, but by an inner logic or necessity. Suddenly I found my feet were set on a path where I could turn neither aside nor back. Processes of thought which had been suspended in early manhood were resumed again and continued in middle age. My earlier conclusions had been true, broadly speaking—there was no going back on that. But had they in fact, as I imagined, disposed of the Church and of Christianity? Was there 'a clean sweep', after all? It seemed not.

Then I began to perceive that the assertions which the Church was making were not vulnerable to the weapons with which I had thought them demolished. It had been a

warfare in which the blows fell on air, in a place where the
antagonist was not standing. History outside the Church
knew nothing of the inner history of the Church's gospel;
but in what sense did the Gospel purport to be history? The
more fixedly one looked, the less it resembled history, the
less it appeared that those who formed it had any notion of
making historical assertions. It had evidently been an
assumption, and one which looked less and less well founded,
to have mistaken for history, and therefore for 'untrue'
history, what was something else altogether. There were
truths and truths—truths lying side by side and not con-
tradicting one another, truths lying above and below and
not destroying one another. Once my misconception of the
nature of the Gospels, a misconception which looked
increasingly crude, began to dissolve, they aroused an
astonishment which grew with repetition and reflection: I
would no more need to fear coming to the end and walking
out empty-handed than the scientist needs to fear getting
to the bottom of the natural universe. The techniques of
criticism and analysis were as powerless to refute the Gospel
as the techniques of scientific investigation are to refute the
material to which they are applied.

At the same time something else was going on. Once got
within the walls, physical and liturgical, of the Church of
England, I was proud enough and English enough to see
that it was a goodly inheritance from which, like a prodigal
son, I had so long deliberately exiled myself. However, like
someone who returns after long absence to an ancestral
home, I looked at the half-familiar scenes with new eyes.
Here was yet another kind of truth which I had not
suspected. For all the wonders of the national church and
its mother tongue, there was no stopping-place there, no rest
for the soles of the feet. I discovered that whoever entered
the south door of a parish church had stepped inside the
Church Universal. The more he laboured to understand and
to render intelligible the inheritance of his own church, the
more plainly he would confront the fact of the Catholic
Church: that the truth of the Gospel and the truth of the
Church, the existence of the Gospel and the existence of

the Church, the knowledge of the Gospel and the knowledge of the Church, are indivisible, and the one unthinkable without the other. I had been compelled to acknowledge a truth that is corporate, and when I had done so, I noticed that the loyalties I had lived with in war and peace had been corporate too.

Perhaps it was at this point that necessity, or it might be called obligation, took a hand. Speaking with the voice of a parish priest, and addressing itself not specially to me but to all who would hear, it proclaimed duty, in terms plain, simple and unapologetic. In particular, it proclaimed the duty of Holy Communion. As I listened, I knew that I no longer had any choice; and in the dawn of an Easter morning I set out for the second time, but now with the experience and purpose of a mature adult, upon the endless journey of exploration of the meaning and content of the Mass.

Once again, I found I had nothing to unlearn but only more, and yet more, to learn. Truth was not so much many-sided, as many-mansioned. The *Golden Bough* and the priest king and the universality of the god slain and eaten— so far from these being a confutation of the crucifixion and its perpetual memorial, they were as necessary to it, though in a different sense, as the Old Testament was to the New. The Holy Communion was not only invulnerable to every other department of human experience and knowledge, but it illuminated them with its own light.

I can end my brief story here; for of the course of my thought and experiences since then the following pages contain a series of markers, which I had occasion to set up along the route. I have arranged them, not quite chrono-logically, in a certain sequence of three groups, though these overlap. In the first I find myself preoccupied with the meaning of the creeds in relation to time, immortality and eternity. The second might be headed 'God and Caesar'. Starting by accepting uncritically the familiar interpretation of that antithesis, I go on first to criticize and then to reject it. This leads directly to the third group, which could be entitled 'The unresolved contradiction'. In one context after another I find no escape from recognizing the dilemma of the Church in the world as irresolvable but essential to its nature.

I shall not need to be told how limited and partial are any insights which these addresses disclose; but one person's partial insight may sometimes be the piece for which someone else was looking.

ENOCH POWELL

1

WHOSOEVER WILL

The Prayer Book commands that at Christmas, Easter, Whitsun and no fewer than ten other feast days there shall be said or sung at Morning Prayer, instead of the Apostles' Creed, a confession of our Christian faith, 'commonly called the Creed of Saint Athanasius'. Though the number of prescribed occasions was not at first so large, this injunction has been part of our law from the very first English Prayer Book.

The creed in question is also, and better, known by its first two words in Latin, *quicunque vult*, 'whosoever will (be saved)'. Its origin is extremely obscure. What is certain about it is that it can have had nothing to do with St Athanasius, but is an entirely Western creed. It is now thought to have originated in Spain or Northern Italy in the fifth century.

The most famous phrases of the creed, in the definition of the Trinity, ('not three incomprehensibles ... but one incomprehensible'), are familiar to countless people who have no idea of their source, and they have been the subject of innumerable allusions and parodies. But the keynote of the creed is the fiercely absolute assertion at the outset 'which (Catholic) faith except everyone do keep whole and undefiled, without doubt he shall perish everlastingly'. The same solemn assertion is repeated in respect to each of the two halves into which the creed divides—the doctrine of the Trinity ('he therefore that will be saved, must thus think of the Trinity') and the doctrine of the incarnation ('it is necessary to everlasting salvation, that he believe rightly the incarnation of our lord Jesus Christ'). It ends on the same note: 'This is the Catholic faith, which except a man believe faithfully he cannot be saved'.

This is what essentially differentiates the Athanasian Creed from the more familiar Apostles' and Nicene Creeds. They define the content of the faith, and refer explicitly to the means of salvation. This alone asserts the faith to be indispensable to salvation.

It is this no doubt which makes the Athanasian Creed unpopular; for unpopular it is, and the injunction that it be read is perhaps (what Shakespeare did *not* mean by), 'more honoured in the breach than the observance'. We find it grotesque that eternal damnation should be attached to ignorance of, not to mention disbelief in, a definition of the Trinity and the incarnation, especially so detailed and difficult a definition. In any case, eternal damnation itself, to 'perish everlastingly', has long been quite out of fashion, something regarded in the light of a period piece, like wax flowers under glass and reminiscent of Victorian Sunday afternoons or black-coated preachers in Welsh chapels. So people think, if they do not actually say, 'Let's skip those pages, they're quite out of date'—or 'spent', as the Parliamentary lawyers would put it.

The proposition I wish to put to you is that the bath water so frequently and all but unthinkingly jettisoned contains a very large and important baby—if not more than one. It is not unusual to discover that when we suppose ourselves to have risen superior to what generations of our predecessors found overwhelmingly significant and self-evident, we are in reality describing our own impoverishment of imagination or of vision. The generations of men who found nothing impossible, on the contrary found something inescapably compelling, in the central assertion of the Athanasian Creed were not unthinking fools in the grip of vulgar superstition, nor were they, with few exceptions, bloodthirsty bigots, intent on forging subtle instruments of dissension and oppression. If their words appear to us to present them in that light, it may be that we have not troubled to translate; for their mental furniture was as different from ours as their language. It may however also be that we are afraid to face what they were able to look upon fearlessly.

Let me then attempt a very rough and approximate translation. It might run somewhat as follows:

> The thoughts we hold about ourselves and our fellows and about our relation to the universe are overwhelmingly important, so important as to make the whole difference between true success in life and failure, between utter happiness and utter misery. Just any thoughts at our own option will not do; they must be thoughts of a particular nature, if they are to have this result. Being each of us unique and bound in by time, our failure, if we fail, cannot be made good, the tape cannot be run back, erased or 'edited'. Once for all, it makes our eternity.

My paraphrase, I know, is terribly free; but it seeks to remove one obstacle to comprehension, at least. It shows the problematic assertion about faith, salvation and damnation as not a threat but a statement. We are wrong if we read the assertion as a threat of punishment, as if it were that anyone failing to get 100 per cent in this examination paper will be taken out and shot. Assuming a tyrant God to be in the writers' minds and filling in the picture with weighing-scales and demons from the later medieval Dooms, we interpret the words accordingly. I suggest we should be over-shooting the mark much less in the other direction if we treat the words as the statement of an equation: to hold the Catholic faith *equals* salvation; to be possessed by a true view of the deity as expressed in the doctrines of the Trinity and the incarnation *is* the life everlasting.

It is overtones of judicial punishment, which we have to make an effort to banish from our mental ear, that also render the time expressions so grotesque and repulsive. We read the words 'everlasting' and 'everlastingly' as if they were the term of a sentence of penal servitude and get them mixed up subconsciously with notions about 'making the punishment fit the crime' or 'getting greater uniformity of sentences in the magistrates' courts'. Heard as a judicial sentence on an offender, the disproportion between an

eternity of punishment and a defect or error of belief in the
brief span of human life strikes us as ludicrous, not to say
unjust. Restated as a proposition not merely of cause and
effect, automatic, inevitable, impersonal, but even of actual
equivalence, the assertion loses its repellent quality, and we
are set free to consider what it is really telling us.

It seems to me that the Creed confronts us with three
facts which we are extremely reluctant to recognize, and to
which the prevalent mood of our age and society renders
us particularly allergic.

The first fact is that Christianity is an intellectual religion.
Some religions are not: their demands can be fulfilled, and
their promises obtained, by actions divorced from thoughts.
Christianity, on the other hand, is a faith which makes
demands upon people's minds, and relates its promises to
the results of mental activity. You do not have to rely on
the Athanasian Creed to verify this. It is stated with
frightening directness in one of the sentences cited before
the burial service: 'He that believeth in me, though he
were dead, yet shall he live; and whosoever liveth and
believeth in me shall never die' (John 11.25). So far as
the connection between belief and salvation is concerned,
the Athanasian Creed goes not a whit beyond that.
Christianity is about the content of a human mind.

From this follows the second fact which we are desperately
anxious to avoid seeing, namely, the possibility, indeed the
probability, the prevalence, of failure. If success, life, salvation—use which term you will—depends on a content of the
mind, then those incapable for any reason of the requisite
mental activity, or of entertaining the essential propositions,
must fail, or die, or be damned, according to the terminology
chosen. Ignorance, incapacity, perversity, the sheer human
propensity to error are sufficient to ensure a high failure
rate.

This again is not something invented for the purpose of
the Athanasian Creed. Over and over again the Christ of
the Gospels asserts that his salvation will not be for all, not
even for the majority, that 'few are chosen' (Matt. 22.14).
We need not involve ourselves here in the theology of

election and pre-destination, to admit that failure—the possibility, probability, prevalence of failure—is asserted by Christianity as a corollary of its assertion that success consists in a mental state.

Throughout two thousand years one expedient after another has been tried in the attempt to modify or avoid this corollary: they range from certain interpretations of infant baptism to the retrospective conversion of Socrates and Virgil to Christianity. But for no generation perhaps has it been so difficult to face this hard saying as our own place and time, with its shibboleth of 'equality of opportunity' and its idolization of 'fair shares'. In a sugary, romantic, cosy religion, suitable to match the welfare state, there would not only be equality of opportunity to be saved, but an insurance scheme thrown in, to ensure that nobody missed salvation just through being born in the wrong place at the wrong time, or not happening to entertain the necessary belief, or being incapable of doing so. It would be a religion in which every story had a happy ending, here or hereafter. There may be, and no doubt are, such religions; but Christianity is not one of them. Christianity is not for us unless we are able to face the fact that failure exists.

What is more, and this is the third fact which the Athanasian Creed will not allow us to evade, failure can be final, absolute and irrevocable. The Creed expresses this by means of the time metaphor—'everlasting salvation', 'he shall perish everlastingly'—that being a convenient, effective and even indispensable way to convey finality. But this assertion of the finality of the success or failure of the individual human soul, the finality (to use the forensic metaphor) of the judgement, is not an invention of the catechists and the creed-writers. The teaching of Christ in the Gospels is saturated with it. This life, and above all the nature of a man's belief and disbelief in this life, determine once for all what he is to all eternity. It is this awful sense of finality which endowed with urgency and earnestness not only the Christianity of the early churches, with their expectation of an imminent second coming, but all Christianity down the ages.

Once more, men have sought means to cushion and shield themselves against having to meet this truth face to face. The comfortable doctrines of purgatory and intercession for the dead attract because they offer some escape from the intolerable finality of judgement on the human life completed. Yet that finality is already implicit in the basic assertion of Christianity that salvation is about belief. Whether or not Macbeth so meant it, the connection is marvellously expressed in that,

> but here, upon this bank and shoal of time,
> we'd jump the life to come; but in these cases
> we still have judgement here.

Indeed we do; for that judgement runs concurrently with the mental act, a judgement continuously pronounced as life itself proceeds.

By this insight the hours of human life, which at most moments seem to us so brief and mean, are endowed with the awe of eternity. This individual, unique atom of self-consciousness subtends the whole universe of space and time.

It is an uncomfortable conviction to live with, a conviction which imposes solemn, almost insupportable responsibility. But here we stand already on the threshold of the *content* of that Catholic faith, 'which except everyone keep whole and undefiled, without doubt he shall perish everlastingly'. I have remained tonight outside that threshold, not purposing more than to suggest that the context and outer framework in which the Athanasian Creed expounds the Catholic faith, so far from being obsolete or repugnant, is there to remind us of certain truths which we dare not forget or blur about the nature of that faith itself.

2

THE RESURRECTION OF THE BODY[1]

When, in reciting the Apostles' Creed, we come to the words, 'the resurrection of the body', I imagine that most of us—if our minds are working at all—take some sort of mental avoiding action. 'The resurrection of the body': too gross, too fantastic, quite unacceptable. It was no doubt all very well for the simple Middle Ages, with their crude notions, to depict in the Dooms painted over chancel arches, actual bodies of the dead rising up at the sound of the trumpet. It is all very well for Stanley Spencer, with malicious realism, to force us to contemplate ordinary men and women literally emerging from their graves. But you and I cannot possibly be so naive.

Maybe we could escape by supposing that some other sort of body altogether may be meant, a body which isn't a body or at any rate which isn't this body? And aren't there one or two texts somewhere in St Paul which seem to mean that? Anyhow, the Nicene Creed only speaks of, 'the resurrection of the dead'; and it is a fact that in the Greek of the first centuries A.D.—unlike classical Greek—the word νεκρός meant not only 'a corpse' but quite simply 'a dead person': so perhaps there's just been a mistranslation?

But all these notions are just subterfuges, and we know in our hearts that they are. The Church is quite outspoken and unambiguous. In the Holy Communion we are told to ask, in the prayer of humble access, 'that our sinful bodies may be made clean by his body', and in the actual delivery of the elements the formula is absolutely uncompromising:

[1] National Association for the Prevention of Tuberculosis service at St Martin's-in-the-Fields, 5 May 1957.

'The body of our Lord Jesus Christ—or the blood (as the case may be)—preserve thy *body* and soul unto everlasting life.' Our bodies and our souls are both to be immortal, or neither is. We are to be saved body and soul, or not at all. Indeed, that this, as the Apostles' Creed plainly has it, is the belief and teaching of the universal Church through the ages, we must wilfully deceive ourselves if we are not to recognize.

Yet there never was a time when such self-deception was less excusable than the present. There have been periods when the antithesis of body and soul was vividly felt and when the evidence to break down that antithesis was lacking. But the modern sciences have smashed the frontier barriers between body and soul irretrievably. The behaviour, the moral qualities, the thoughts, beliefs, and opinions, everything which characterized the spiritual part of a man—to use theological terms, everything which marked a soul for damnation or salvation—has been found to have a physical basis, and to be capable of manipulation and alteration by physical means. We can change a man's moral character by an operation; we can express a state of mind in chemical and in electrical terms; we can trace with precision and confidence the relation of cause and effect between physiological conditions and mental and moral acts. Body and soul have in truth become for us, as in the formula of the Eucharist, an indissoluble unity, two aspects and expressions of one and the same object.

The escape route of belief in the immortality of an abstract disembodied soul is for us cut off. It was in truth an easy belief only because it could be a vague belief, demanding no sharp precision of thought nor severe effort of mind. But we in our day must stand and make our choice and give our answer in the open: if 'resurrection', if 'everlasting life', if 'the life of the world to come' means anything at all, it must mean something which can be as true of the body as of the soul. Does it mean anything, or nothing?

The scrap of humanity which comes into the world with all the chances loaded against its health and survival; the congenitally defective who all their lives will be objects of pity and revulsion and a burden to those who care for them;

the long, losing fight for the life of a victim of tuberculosis or cancer; hardest of all, paradoxically, the patient recovered and sent back into the world for a shorter or longer span but in the end to be as though he had never recovered and had never existed; and, around and above it all, this huge apparatus of knowledge, resources, skill and effort which society has laboriously erected for the succouring of its members—does it have a meaning, or does it not?

The question will not be suppressed; for unless the individual human entity of body and soul, the most deformed, imperfect, or disease-ridden no less than the healthiest and most complete, the meanest no less than the noblest, has an absolute meaning and value, immune from the 'changes and chances' of the world, then indeed all nursing is merely 'vanity and vexation of spirit'. As the nurse asks in Tennyson's poem, 'The Children's Hospital':

O how could I serve in the wards if the hope of the world were a lie,
How could I bear with the sights and the loathsome smells of disease?

It is in fact the same question as before: does 'resurrection', 'everlasting life', the 'life of the world to come' have a meaning at all, a meaning as true of the body as of the soul?

It is this question which the Church answers when it teaches us that the Word which created the universe became flesh and dwelt among us, became manifest, that is to say, not in some perfect archetype of humanity but in the actual flesh with its inheritance of diseases and imperfections and deformities. The Church answers the question when it teaches that the apparent defeat of the Word made flesh was in truth his victory, and his apparent death in truth immortality. The Church answers the question when it denies the limitations of time and space, and causes the drama of the incarnation, crucifixion and resurrection, unique but timeless, to be repeated for ever, in all ages and throughout the world. The Church answers the question when it says through our own lips, in the words of the Apostles' Creed, 'I believe in the resurrection of the body'.

3

ALPHA AND OMEGA[1]

I am Alpha and Omega, the beginning and the ending, saith the Lord, which is and which was and which is to come (Rev. 1.8).

In these words St John is trying to express, as far as human words can, the fact that God is outside and beyond *time*: God, he says, contains in himself both beginning and end (Alpha and Omega, 'A to Z', as we should say); he contains in himself the past ('which was'), the present ('which is') and the future ('which is to come').

Holidays are a good opportunity for thinking a little about time. On holiday we may not be any less busy or occupied than when we are at home and at work—in fact, given decent weather, we probably intend to be very fully occupied indeed—but for a week or two the rhythm of our lives is altered. We are doing different things, in different places and to a different programme; and this break in the rhythm, or repetition, of our lives gives us the chance to pause a moment and look at ourselves, as it were, from the outside.

One thought that must strike us is how dominated our lives are by *time*. Time—we cannot escape from it. 'Have I time to catch the train?'—'time to write this before the mail goes?'—'time to get all the work done before the children come back from school?' We are always worrying about time, time in minutes and hours which regulates our day; time in months and years, which measures the span of our lives. 'Is there *time* to get married and have a family before it is too late?' asks the young, but no longer very young, woman. 'Have I time to build up this concern before I

[1] Butlin's Holiday Camp, Clacton, 6 August 1960.

come to retire?' asks the middle-aged businessman. 'Have I time,' asks the junior minister, 'to work my way into the Cabinet before I get too old and am dropped?' Time, always time!

Some of our biggest mistakes, and some of our worst sins, are committed because of time, because of this feeling that time is breathing down our necks. 'An old man in a hurry', his critics used to say about Mr Gladstone; but young men, as well as old, can be in too much of a hurry and break the laws of man and the laws of God because they 'hear Time's winged chariot hurrying near'. Fraud—to get rich quick; immorality—to snatch enjoyment quick; hatred and ambition—to get power quick.

Now, we cannot escape out of time, because (as the hymn has it) we are the 'sons of time': our human capacities can only understand the world about us and our own lives in it in terms of time. But man cannot be happy, nor can he be good, unless in some way he frees himself from the mastery of time and comes to see that there is a truth and a reality beyond its reach.

This lesson the Church is teaching us, if we will but listen, in a hundred different voices: her doctrines and her sacraments can only be understood if we see that they are a denial of time or, if you like, a victory over time.

Christianity, they say, is an historical religion, and so it is: we date the birth of Christ; we date the crucifixion; the first three Gospels are all careful to insert a definite date very near the beginning. But Christianity also proceeds to deny and to destroy time: 'Before Abraham was, I am,' says Christ to the astonished Jews (John 8.58); 'Lo, I am with you alway, even unto the end of the world', says Christ to his disciples (Matt. 28.20); and he promises to his believers that he has given them the same power to triumph over time as he has himself: 'He that believeth in me, though he were dead, yet shall he live; and whosoever liveth and believeth in me shall never die' (John 11.25). The words are like a slap in the face to time, to the idea of a sequence in which life and existence are followed by death and annihilation.

So we make difficulties, or impossibilities, for ourselves by insisting upon time. We see our parents and our friends grow old and die, and cannot imagine to ourselves the fact that they are nevertheless alive in Christ because we try to think of them as going on along the same time-scale; and so the question whether they live to be re-united with us as they were in youth, or as they were in middle or old age, or as they were at the moment of a perhaps painful and disfiguring death presents itself to us, grotesque and un-answerable. The trouble lies in our attempting to introduce the thought of time into truths which are a denial of time.

We can make the same mistake the other way round. Just as we can fail to realize that with God, 'a thousand ages ... are like an evening gone', we can also fail to realize that there can be eternity in an instant. Without this, the facts of conversion and salvation and the sacrament of baptism do not mean to us what they should. When the nobleman came to ask Jesus to heal his son and Jesus replied: 'Go thy way; thy son liveth', the Gospel relates that on returning home he found that his son had recovered in the instant in which Jesus had said to him, 'thy son liveth', and he himself had believed it—in a flash the faith of the father had altered, between one second and the next, the whole course of existence and had made the difference between life and death, not merely for himself but for his son.[2]

The Christian gets into hopeless difficulties if he fails to hear this message. Western Christendom tore itself in two, committed endless cruelties and shed oceans of blood in the dispute between Catholic and Protestant, which turned very largely on the question of what happens on the altar at Holy Communion: is it in some sense the actual present sacrifice of the Redeemer or a commemoration of his past sacrifice at Calvary? The question, you see, is posed, in terms of *time*, upon that distinction between past and present which we human beings cannot avoid in thought or speech but which is non-existent in God. So the thing about which we dispute

<hr>

[2] John 4.50–53. I have omitted the interpolated words, 'and his whole household', which destroy the meaning of the passage. They were inserted to provide an antithesis to, 'he himself', which had been deprived of its original antithesis, 'Jesus', by mispunctuation.

and even fight is something to which Christianity denies ultimate reality.

It is like the old ballad about the knight killed in battle, who asked and received forgiveness during the actual second or two while he was falling from his horse:

> Betwixt the saddle and the ground
> Mercy he sought, mercy he found.

If time has no real existence, eternity can be as an instant and an instant can be as eternity; and so we are able to believe, and believe without absurdity, that in the sacrament of baptism, by an act of our belief, a change comes about so sharp and so profound that St Paul described it as being like the difference between life and death.

This denial and flouting of time by Christianity is a 'hard saying'. I have not found it easy to put into words these thoughts. It is a harder thing still to believe and to live. We cannot go back home and stop the grandfather clock in the entrance hall or the time-clock at the factory, and suppose that we shall then live happily ever after. As human beings we are as subject to time as we are to death or to sin, nor can we ever by ourselves break clean loose from the one any more than from the others. What *is* possible is by the help of our faith to attain to an attitude towards time, a habit and way of thinking about it, which will more and more set us free from its mastery. We shall still have to catch that train; we shall still try to beat the years and get the most we can from them in our private lives, in our work and business, in our careers. But the fear and the grudge, the temptation and the sin, can be taken out of it.

For this, as for all else that concerns us as human souls, we need, and we possess, a link between ourselves and God. What would be impossible to man confronting the Timeless and Omnipotent alone, becomes possible to him through the means of Christ and his Church. St Paul gives this answer to the problem of time, as to other problems, in that great passage (Rom. 8.39) where he says that neither, 'height nor depth'—that is, our human conception of space—'nor things present nor things to come'—that is the human con-

ception of time—'shall be able to separate us from the love
of God which is in Christ Jesus our Lord'. Into that last
phrase is concentrated the truth which sets us free. Through
Christ we have the knowledge, and the knowledge that we
have the love, of that God, 'which is, and which was, and
which is to come'.

4

TWO MASTERS[1]

I want to take not one text, but two. The first is Matt. 22.21:
'Then saith he unto them, Render therefore unto Caesar
the things which are Caesar's; and unto God the things that
are God's.' The other text is Matt. 6.24: 'No man can
serve two masters; for either he will hate the one, and love
the other; or else he will hold to the one, and despise the
other. He cannot serve God and Mammon.'

Our Lord, as we are permitted to see him in the Gospels,
is not the founder of a philosophical school, handing down
to his disciples and hearers, in a carefully prepared series of
lectures, some complete and rounded system, with all difficulties and objections smoothed away and no contradictions
or inconsistencies left between one part of it and another.
So we often find different sayings of Jesus which plant us
firmly on the horns of a dilemma. The two sayings which
I quoted just now are an example of this. If no man can
serve two masters, he cannot serve God and Caesar any
more than God and Mammon; it is not only that their
demands may and do conflict: they belong to different
worlds, to different orders of things. We cannot obey the
one injunction without breaking the other.

There *is* a paradox here, no use denying it. But there is
intended to be a paradox. For this is part of the great
paradox of mankind itself, its partaking of two natures
and belonging to two worlds. The 'hard sayings' of our Lord
are hard, and his paradoxes are real, because they are
addressed to beings such as we are. Unless we could

[1] A sermon preached at a service for the Friends of the Hospitals at
Oswestry Parish Church, 21 October 1962.

renounce one side of our nature completely and resign altogether from the service of God—and I doubt if the most wicked and depraved can ever quite do that—then we must acknowledge that this dilemma, this tension, this contradiction, is an inseparable accompaniment of our existence itself.

This is hospital Sunday, and we in this church this afternoon are all concerned in one way or another with the hospital service. Now the hospital service in this country is provided, financed and organized by Caesar; for Caesar means the state, the impersonal and secular state, and this is a *state* hospital service—almost exclusively so—within the larger framework of a *state* health service. For every single act of omission or commission in every one of our hospitals, responsibility is taken by, and owed to, the state. Practically every penny which is spent on building our hospitals and on running them is state financed: it is the 'tribute money', exacted by Caesar and expended by Caesar. I ought to know; for I happen momentarily to be the steward whose duty it is to stand before Caesar and render account to him.

Small wonder if Caesar pervades every branch and aspect of the service. The service itself is of necessity a political issue, and political parties study how its excellencies or its deficiencies, real or otherwise, can be used to triumph over their adversaries and win votes, or to damage and injure their opponents' reputation and thrust them from their places. No misfortune, no suffering, no individual fate is sacred from being thrown as a missile in the political battle. All in the service are in Caesar's pay—the cash nexus, as the older economists used to say—and it is no pleasant business when Caesar and his servants get to bargaining about their money: 'the uttermost farthing', plus or minus, becomes the absorbing object of interest and endeavour to bureaucrat and professional alike. If the state has to answer for half a million persons who render the service and a whole nation which receives it, the state's commands must be obeyed, and its channels of communication must be kept open, through a great hierarchy and network, reporting, checking and counter-checking.

All this is true and real, so far as it goes; but having looked on that picture, now look on this. A service in which political opponents work side by side for its improvement and even rival spokesmen share aspirations for advance; a service in the administration of which hundreds of people give lavishly of their time and effort without a penny of pay or a thought of recognition; a service where whole professions recognize a duty to the patient with which they would allow no other consideration to interfere; a service for which, in sheer affection, countless people throughout the land demand to add their own mite of cash or endeavour to all that Caesar's hundreds of millions of gold can buy. And something more—how comes it that the state, this cold, impersonal, soulless state, concerned itself with a hospital service at all?

Not because it pays, not because there is some net economic gain to be reaped from providing a free, universal, and comprehensive health service. That rather sordid fallacy has been thoroughly exploded. A service which never brings the economic value of the patient or the cost of the treatment into its assignment of priorities, a service of which some of the most vigorously developing elements are devoted to the treatment and care of the old and of the severely handicapped in body and mind—whatever the motive and impulse behind the creation and maintenance of such a service, it is certainly not economic calculation or the self-interest of Caesar. On the contrary it arises from an inner compulsion which we try, but fail, to describe by such epithets as 'humanitarian', or 'altruistic', or 'progressive'. There are things which mankind does, or strives to do, because, in Luther's words, 'God help me, I can no other'.

My critics in the House of Commons have sometimes, when in the mood to pay me a back-handed, curate's egg sort of compliment, been pleased to call me Jekyll and Hyde. But indeed it is not only the Minister of Health who is Jekyll and Hyde. The state hospital service and the National Health Service itself are Jekyll and Hyde. Caesar, the cold, impersonal, materialistic state, has, Janus-like, another face: the community, like its individual members, partakes of two natures and belongs to two worlds. We in this country perhaps more than others have never been willing to admit that the state is wholly secular but have always sensed, Anglicans and non-Anglicans alike, that it must somehow be the Church as well, and that it cannot, any more than ourselves, be described or explained in terms of one world only.

We see the paradox in visible form, those who all the day long 'render unto Caesar the things that are Caesar's' come here to confess the truth that 'no man can serve two masters' and to acknowledge the mystical commandment of God, only fulfillable by his inspiration, to 'love thy neighbour as thyself' (Matt. 22.37). We cannot as individuals ever wholly escape from the contradictions of our nature; but we believe that nevertheless we can emphasize and find help to emphasize the part of it which we call immortal, and that we ourselves can thus be altered. The hospital service cannot ever wholly escape from the nature of a state institution or put off its characteristics as such: we shall still make politics with it, still count the cost of it on a parliamentary vote, still drive hard bargains in it, still administer it by rule and line. Yet we believe that by a livelier and stronger consciousness of the other meaning and context to all that we do, it too can be altered.

5

GOD AND CAESAR

Dialogue with Malcolm Muggeridge[1]

MUGGERIDGE
Enoch, I find it very strange to be standing here in this
pulpit with you in the other pulpit. I remember so vividly
when I first set eyes on you, thirty years ago now. You had
just put your uniform on, I think, as an officer, and you had
a rather large moustache of the sort that used to be called
a soup-strainer, which was, you explained to me afterwards,
because you were going through a phase of tremendous
fascination with Nietzsche. I realized even then that you
were a very unusual person. But now thirty years later you
find yourself in the eyes of some people a man of destiny,
and in the eyes of other people a sort of black figure in the
political spectrum; no doubt, in the eyes of some of your
political colleagues, what Churchill said about Aneurin
Bevan in the war—a nuisance.

POWELL
He said 'a squalid nuisance'.

MUGGERIDGE
I spared the word.

POWELL
Let's have it whole.

MUGGERIDGE
This is, after all, a church and if there were going to be a
text and a reading, I should have taken it from the passage
in St Matthew's Gospel (22.15) where the rather cunning
Pharisees come to our Lord and ask him whether they

[1] St Mary-le-Bow, Cheapside, London, 15 December 1970.

should pay tribute to Caesar. And our Lord says: 'Then show me a penny'. He points to the figure of Caesar on the penny and makes the very interesting remark that they should render unto Caesar the things that are Caesar's and unto God the things that are God's. I feel that for someone like you this question of what is due to God and what is due to Caesar is a basic question.

POWELL

I think that as with so many sayings and parables, we read too hastily what is actually written, and the result of doing that is that we make it much shallower than it really is. The question that was asked, as you said, is: 'Is it lawful to pay tribute to Caesar?' It was a political question. It was arguably a legal question. It was arguably an economic question. Is income tax too high at 7s. 9d. in the pound? In view of the history of the Jewish people, have we a duty of rebellion? A series of economic and political questions was implicit in the one question which was put to Christ. And when he said: 'Render unto Caesar the things that are Caesar's,' I do not believe that he was answering the question. He was not saying, yes of course you must pay your taxes; yes of course you must play your part, whatever you consider it to be, as a citizen or a Roman subject. As I understand it, he was refusing to answer the question. He was in fact saying, you are asking me a question which to me is perfectly irrelevant; therefore I cannot deduce the answer from anything that I have come to do or anything that I have come to tell you. He was denying in the most precise manner the relevance, if I may risk that word, of his mission to politics, to economics. He was saying, you cannot deduce from anything that I have to say what should be the level of tribute or what should be the political relationship between Rome and Judaea. He was denying the deducibility of conclusions in that sphere.

MUGGERIDGE

You would accept, I'm sure, that every single person living in this world owes something to God. Are you conscious yourself that there are things that you owe to God which can be distinguished from what you owe to men or to the state?

POWELL

The word 'distinguished', I feel, puts it too mildly. It seems to me rather that there are two completely different worlds, both present in oneself, which overlie one another or run parallel. There is no neat division and distinction between the religious duty and the civic duty. Indeed, the religious duty is 100 per cent. I find this over and over again asserted by Christ and misheard—because it is so painful to hear it— by us. As in the answer to the rich young ruler who asked what he should do to inherit eternal life (Matt. 19.16). He wasn't told to be charitable, he wasn't told to practise more charity, he was told to divest himself of everything. This seems to me to be one of the characteristics of Christianity, the absoluteness and exclusiveness of its claim and there- fore—I'm again taking a risk with this word—the deliberate impracticability of its claim. We are made to live in the face of an impossible demand all the time.

MUGGERIDGE

So there's a contradiction. On the one hand a duty to God and on the other hand a duty as a citizen, as a politician, as a man. Which do you choose?

POWELL

I live in both worlds. These are both parts of a human being, of a human personality. They live side by side—if you like, they are irreconcilable. I am told, for instance, to love my neighbour as myself (Matt. 22.37) not just to love my neigh- bour. We commonly misunderstand this. I am told to do that which no human being can do, which the nature of a human prevents him from doing: namely, loving someone else as himself. Yet I am constantly reminded of this im- possible demand which is placed upon me by the other part of my nature as revealed, if you like, or as symbolized—no, these are weak words, unsatisfactory words—by Christ.

MUGGERIDGE

Then you would say there's a sort of schizophrenia in living here, that we must be two men, not one man.

POWELL
But we *are* two men.

MUGGERIDGE
We are two men. But is there no relationship between those
two men? Let's consider concrete things. You, as a politician,
pursue power. Would that be true? The quest of politics
is power.

POWELL
It's not quite so crude as it's commonly represented, but I'll
let you get away with that.

MUGGERIDGE
No, I don't want to get away with it, Enoch. I want it to be
true. In pursuing power, you have to do things and accept
things which, if we consider these two men inside us, would
be abhorrent to the other man. Is that right?

POWELL
If you mean one has to do things which offend against
morality, against one's sense of what is fair, just, right,
truthful, I wouldn't concede that.

MUGGERIDGE
No, I wasn't meaning that.

POWELL
But if you mean one has to live a life which does not fulfil
the absolute commandments, the searching commandments,
which are placed upon us by Christ and the Church, yes.

MUGGERIDGE
Then what is the purpose of those commands? Is it that we
should ignore them, that we should say, well, this is a
department of life in which they don't apply?

POWELL
There are many sides to a man. There is, for example, or
can be, an artistic side: part of a man's nature may vibrate
to greatness in various forms of art. I would find it very hard
to say that a man, of whose nature the other sides were

open and cultivated, would not be different, and, I would be obliged to say, better, as a politician. Yet I could not say, because he has those other sides of his nature open and developed, therefore he votes for or against this Bill; therefore he proposes this or that amendment; therefore he belongs to the Labour Party or the Conservative Party. I could not draw a direct deduction from the one aspect of the man to the other. Similarly, it seems to me impossible to deny that a man upon whom there are borne in day by day and week by week, these demands, perfections, ultimates, of which the Church speaks, is not going to be different somehow in his life as a politician from what he otherwise would be. All the same I'm helpless if you say, well, tell me, give me an example; tell me how he would decide differently on the legislation and policies of the present session. I cannot. Of course I can tell you that over and over again, and often in the course of a day, I am conscious in my life as a politician of committing the sins of hatred, of envy, of malice; and I am conscious of the command operating, to some extent at any rate, upon my nature which not merely forbids these things but equates them with death. Therefore I must hope that as a man amongst men I will be that much nearer—I'm accepting your view of approximation—to what I am required to be than otherwise would be the case.

MUGGERIDGE

If Christianity means anything at all, it means this sense of belonging to a family whose father is God, a family whose unity lies in a common love of their creator. Anything which separated human beings, which put human beings into different categories, which created conflicts and hatred between human beings, would in my estimation be offending against the Christian faith and turning one's back on the mission that brought its founder into this world. Take, for instance, the social system which exists in South Africa, called apartheid. All social systems, I agree with you, are unjust. On the other hand, there you have a society based on a definite theory of separation, a specific theory that the quality of one man is different from the quality of another man. Would you not agree that that theory is *per se* contrary to the Christian religion?

POWELL

But in many contexts we agree that one person is inferior in quality to another.

MUGGERIDGE

No, Enoch.

POWELL

What are examinations about?

MUGGERIDGE

We may consider that one man is more intelligent than another, is more beautiful than another, more athletic than another. But in so far as we accept this Christian notion of men as a family, there can lie in that no sense of an intrinsic difference or inferiority.

POWELL

But that is a supernatural family: it is the family to which we belong by reason of being all equally mortal or all equally in need of redemption.

MUGGERIDGE

All children of God.

POWELL

All children of God in the sense that we have, of all creation, a unique perception of the Creator. But what can I deduce from that as to the treatment of the differences which do exist between men, differences of quality, to which presumably some differences of function must correspond?

MUGGERIDGE

This is a system of living which presupposes an intrinsic separation between people of different races, an intrinsic inferiority on the part of one in relation to the other: can that be regarded as a Christian way of life?

POWELL

I'll certainly come to the specific case you've put to me. It seems to me to depend upon motive. Let me suppose that a person or a party acts in a particular way because he wishes to promote hatred between men, because he desires that there shall be conflict and bloodshed between them. Then this must be irreconcilable—whatever I've said about contradictions and impossibilities—with the duty of a Christian. But let us suppose that, using his judgement and observation as best he can, he concludes that the risk of hatred, bloodshed, violence is minimized by separation— I'm not saying that he's right, but let us suppose that that is his view and his conclusion—then how can you say that he is acting contrary to the basic requirements of the Christian faith by pursuing and promoting policies which in his view minimize the risk of hatred and conflict?

MUGGERIDGE

Again you're taking the empirical view. I want to know whether it can be in God's will that one of his created creatures should regard another of his created creatures for any reason, even for the maintenance of law and order, as separate from him, as ultimately his inferior?

POWELL

I think you've confused inferior and separate. For example, the arguments for separation—I don't necessarily accept them—would be just as valid if those who were to be separated were regarded as superior.

MUGGERIDGE

Don't let's quibble, because they're not. They're regarded as inferiors.

POWELL

I'm not quibbling at all. The theory of separation rests upon difference and is not concerned with inferiority or superiority.

MUGGERIDGE

You first became famous in this country for making certain statements about the situation that had arisen here over the

Asian and African immigrants who have come to live in this country. I personally accept that that was done in complete good faith, that it presented itself to you, particularly in your constituency, as a very serious problem about which it was your duty to speak up. But in the course of speaking up, by virtue of the very intensity with which you presented this problem to your fellow countrymen, would you not agree that you ran the risk of stirring up this sense of fear and hatred which we would both agree are not part of a Christian's duty?

POWELL

We all run risks in real life and in politics; but if I thought that feelings of fear and hatred would not exist and would not grow and would not produce their poisoned fruit if I kept silent, then I would keep silent. We have to go back here again to two things. First, to motive; but you haven't challenged motive—so I leave that. Then, to judgement; but how am I helped in the judgement of an actual situation and of how it is likely to develop by the absolute requirements of Christianity? I have to decide what the dangers are, how they are likely to develop, the conditions under which they will become real. If I allow myself, in deciding that, to substitute wish for prediction, hope for genuine judgement, what good am I doing?

MUGGERIDGE

I think there we have to go back to this question of what is due to God and what is due to Caesar. What is due to God is our love, of him and of one another. Therefore, if in your activities as a politician—and particularly in the field I'm talking about, where the eloquence and intensity and power of your character have been so clearly manifested—if there has been not enough recognition of what is due to God, and too much recognition of what is due to Caesar, whose service, of course, is power, then I think you offend.

POWELL

No, this won't do. The duty to God is of course an absolute, and, as I've said, ultimately unfulfillable. To love one's neighbour as oneself is something which by definition is impossible: it's the denial of selfhood. The Kingdom of heaven is one in which there is neither bond nor free, neither man nor woman, where these distinctions do not exist at all. But in Caesar's world I live in a world in which these distinctions do exist, and in which harm can be brought by politicians upon their fellow citizens by failure of foresight, by failing to detect dangers and provide against them while there is still time, even though those dangers may spring from the evil of men's hearts. If a neighbouring country is arming in order to conquer and embody our country in its own, then the motives which lie behind that are presumably of an evil character. They arise from the evil in men's nature. But I'm not entitled to say: 'Oh, but I mustn't assume that mankind will be filled with such horrible ambitions as that they should actually take up arms and surge across our frontiers. I must not argue that my fellow citizens should rearm or that they should join in alliances designed to produce a balance of power.' If I did that, I should be betraying the trust which in this world is placed in me as a politician by those whom I represent. I have to live in Caesar's world with the realities of Caesar's world. There is not a sharing-out: so much to Caesar and so much to God. They live side by side and in continual conflict. The fact that they are in continual conflict is no justification for me being a bad or incompetent emperor or a stupid centurion.

MUGGERIDGE
Would you consider yourself to be essentially a religious man? I remember hearing you once say that you could easily imagine yourself having been a monk—though I think you would have soon become the abbot.

POWELL
I think this side of my nature is sufficiently pronounced for me to be aware that I have to feed it, have to try to satisfy it. I am aware in relation to religion, of a sensation which is like that of being hungry, as one can be aware of a similar sensation in relation to poetry or music.

MUGGERIDGE
What are you hungering for?

POWELL
I'm hungering to hear, to be told, and to receive, things
which I don't know where to find elsewhere, and which I
feel I shall be the poorer if I don't hear and receive, and
which I believe in some sense I shall die if I don't have.
That's vague—I'm sorry. When one talks of music, one has
to talk in musical terms, and when you talk of religion you
must talk in religious terms.

MUGGERIDGE
Another thing I remember very well is your talking of
when you went to India during the war, and saying how
dazzled and infatuated you were by this Indian empire,
which of course was a very remarkable thing; and how even
being viceroy would perhaps have figured among your very
legitimate ambitions. Well, that empire is gone in the short
time that's elapsed between then and now. That post, that
might have fulfilled your ambitions, no longer exists. People
have forgotten there ever were viceroys. If you continue in
such pursuits, won't this hunger, that I know is in you, be
offended to the point at which there will be a real conflict?

POWELL
There *is* a real conflict. I think there always is in every
religious person, and is bound to be. Of course, I cannot
prophesy that there could not come a moment and circumstances in which one would leave all. But let's not make it
easy for ourselves by failing to recognize that the choice *is*
one of all or nothing. The choice, again, is that which was
put to the rich young ruler, leave all and follow me, that is
the way to inherit eternal life. Now, one *can* deliberately
leave all; but very few do, and you put to me the paradox
that those who hear and vibrate to that injunction to
the rich young ruler, nevertheless remain in Caesar's world
and live out their lives seeking Caesar's prizes. How do you
expect this to be reconciled—except in the Kingdom of God
on earth?

6

UNTO THIS LAST

'I will give unto this last even as unto thee' (Matt. 20.14).
The famous sentence from which Ruskin took the title of
one of his essays is from the parable of the labourers in the
vineyard. At the end of the day's work the master gives the
same wages to those who have worked only the last hour
as to those, 'which have borne the burden and heat of the
day'. To a member of this latter group who expostulates,
the master retorts: 'Is it not lawful for me to do what I
will with mine own? Is thine eye evil because I am good?'

By no manner of contrivance can economic sense be
made out of the master's behaviour. If the same price is to
be paid for a small as for a large amount of effort, all
economic activity, all buying and selling, all markets,
would be brought to a standstill. In real life the employer
would find that, if this was what he wanted to 'do with his
own', he simply could not do it: for example, the next
day, all the hands would have withheld their labour until
the last hour.

But the point of the parable is precisely that it is *not*
economics. The master of the vineyard is God himself, in
whose sight the efforts of all are of equal value, and that
value he chooses to put upon them by his own free will.
The vineyard is not an earthly society, but a theocracy. In
fact, the parable is prefaced, as so many are, with the words,
'the Kingdom of heaven is like unto . . .'.

The parable may be taken as a type of the difficulty which
we experience when we try to apply the words of the
Church's founder to the activities of our lives in society. At
first sight some of the teachings appear to have a practical,

perhaps economic, perhaps political, content. Then on examination they prove to be deliberately—startlingly—impractical, uneconomic, unpolitical. They are paradoxes, the sort of paradoxes produced by the intersection of two worlds, the natural and the supernatural, the time-bound and the timeless.

The commands of Christ to his disciples to 'take no thought for the morrow' (Matt. 6.34), to leave wife and children, etc. are commands which are meant literally, but from which we instantly claim exemption, on the grounds that we are not volunteering to be apostles, or that these rules only apply to the officers, or that that sort of thing is only taken seriously by visionaries or mendicant friars. But it is in vain that we thus attempt to shuffle out of the dilemma, and to escape from the grip of the paradox in which the teaching of the Saviour has imprisoned us. His simplest and most general injunctions are inherently unrealizable.

The command 'to love thy neighbour as thyself' (Matt. 27.39) is commonly misheard, not without assistance from the parable of the good Samaritan, to which it has got itself fortuitously attached in the textual tradition of the one Gospel where that parable occurs (Luke 10.27). We all do a spot of hospital work or charitable endeavour from time to time. There is nothing essentially out of our reach in the Samaritan's behaviour. It was perfectly human as well as humane, and indeed nothing in the narrative suggests that it was more. But the command 'to love thy neighbour as thyself' means exactly what it says, something humanly unattainable, equivalent to the extinction of self-love in the most far-reaching sense. The pursuit of advantage, the instinct of self-preservation itself, are integral to the mechanics of human existence in society; and even when they are apparently suspended, it is on behalf of a person, an institution or indeed the society itself as a whole, with which the individual identifies himself. Even to 'lay down one's life for the brethren' (1 John 3.16) falls short of the commandment, unless 'the brethren' is co-extensive with humanity—and there is only one instance of that upon record.

The dilemma is not solved by the attempt to combine

opposites: 'I fight, but do not break the Queensberry rules; I endeavour to enrich myself and my family, but do not forget to make substantial contributions to charity; I aspire to keep my party and myself in office, but I refrain from personal attacks and deliberate misrepresentations; I try to maximize my firm's profits, but do not squeeze out my competitors by threats or conspiracy.' When the young man who had great possessions inquired what to do to be saved, he was not told to step up his almsgiving or put his money into fixed-rate Roman Imperial securities instead of speculating on the commodity market. He was told to sell *all*, repeat *all*, his goods. The answer of Christianity to the boast of fulfilling the requirements of ordinary social morality— the Queensberry rules, the fair competition, truthfulness, honesty, and the rest—is brutal and direct: 'When ye shall have done all those things which are commanded you, say, "We are unprofitable servants"' (Luke 17.10). St Paul in the famous passage about charity links this answer to the commandment of love and gives it an even sharper point than that which wounded the young man with great possessions: 'Though I bestow all my goods to feed the poor, and though I give my body to be burned' (or should it be, 'sold'[1]?) 'it profiteth me nothing' (1 Cor. 13.3).

It is not, therefore, surprising, that efforts to deduce a code of business ethics or of political conduct from our Lord's teaching have proved unsuccessful or have convinced only those who were determined to find the particular answer that they wanted. It is not surprising that those who looked at the early Church for a pattern of political organization found, to their disappointment, an other-worldly society living in immediate expectation of the second coming. There are no logical bridges which lead across the gulf between the assertions of Christianity and the conduct of the world's business. How different in this respect, and how much more comfortable, are the commandments of the

---

[1] The passage requires a climax; and the only gift left to give after disposing of all one's possessions, is one's person, which can be sold for slavery and the proceeds donated. 'To be sold', $\pi\rho\alpha\theta\dot{\eta}\sigma o\mu\alpha\iota$, is confused with $\kappa\alpha\nu\theta\dot{\eta}\sigma o\mu\alpha\varsigma$, 'to be burned', which would then have been displaced by its gloss, the synonym, $\kappa\alpha\nu\theta\dot{\eta}\sigma o\mu\alpha\iota$.

Old Testament. Though, as St Paul says (Gal. 3.22), they 'concluded all under sin,' at least here are detailed prescriptions—literally the moral and political code of a nation—all neatly set out, and anyone can set about attempting to observe them in everyday life. When we have allowed ourselves to eliminate those requirements which we identify as 'local and private' (as we say in Parliament about certain classes of legislation) and those further requirements which are hopelessly inconvenient and which we regard as obsolete or (again in Parliamentary terms) 'spent', there remains a system of social morality which is not inherently impracticable in the work-a-day world of business or government.

The impracticability, the dilemma, the dividing 'sword' (Matt. 10.34) was revealed by Christianity to just that work-a-day world which was unconscious of it. It was that other world, that supernatural world of the impossibilities, which the scribes and Pharisees could not or would not see. The reply to their question about the tribute-money (p. 26) is absolutely and uncompromisingly a-political. The questions of national self-determination, the right of the Jews to live as a free people, the legitimacy of foreign rule imposed by force, are treated as if they did not exist. The nature and character, the morality and the principles, of Caesar and his *imperium* are irrelevant: the reply would have been the same under Marcus Aurelius, or Commodus, or Heliogabalus, as it was under Tiberius. 'Fear God. Honour the king' (1 Peter 2.17) sounds in the familiar Authorized version so homely to our ears that we instinctively wonder if someone has forgotten to correct 'king' to 'queen' since 1952 in the church copy. But St Peter's injunction covers, and is meant to cover, Hitler equally with Nero and with our most gracious sovereign lady.

There is no escaping this dilemma, this dichotomy, except by self-deception; for the dilemma and the dichotomy are rooted in the nature of man himself, and therefore in the nature of man in society. We do live a double existence—one existence to which Caesar is irrelevant, and another where we fight for or against him, argue about him, reform him, serve him—because we have a double nature. We go through our lives with these incompatible worlds both present at once in our mind and consciousness—knowing and believing that 'he that findeth his life shall lose it' (Matt. 10.39) and at the same time taking desperate pains not to lose it all the same.

The two worlds lie parallel, the two lives are lived simultaneously. What communication is there between the two, what influence of one upon the other? It seems to me that we are equally guilty of the great denial if we pretend that the intercommunication is logical, ascertainable, visible, demonstrable, as if we insist that, since no intercommunication can be logical, ascertainable, visible, demonstrable, therefore that other truth is irrelevant or (as it was once said) 'unto the Jews a stumbling block, and unto the Greeks foolishness' (1 Cor. 1.23). If religion is about faith, then faith lies in this, to be able to live with and in the dilemma of human nature and to assert it defiantly, which is also to assert it triumphantly.

7

THE CHURCH AND
THE WORK OF THE WORLD

I

Once when I was in friendly disputation in a City church it happened that much of the dialogue turned upon the narrative of Christ and the tribute money, and its concluding words: 'Render unto Caesar the things which are Caesar's, and unto God the things that are God's' (Matt. 22.15). The more we wrestled with it, the deeper our difficulties became, and afterwards I found that I went on pondering about it. That antithesis, which thousands of millions of human beings have quoted—it was not only puzzling; it was wrong, dead wrong. Surely, I thought, Christ could not have said it? So I looked again; and I saw that he had not.

Look at the passage, and you also will see the same.

Then went the Pharisees, and took counsel how they might entangle him in his talk. And they sent out unto him their disciples ... saying, Master, we know that thou art true, and teachest the way of God in truth, neither carest thou for any man.... Tell us therefore, What thinkest thou? Is it lawful to give tribute unto Caesar, or not? But Jesus perceived their wickedness, and said, Why tempt ye me, ye hypocrites? Show me the tribute money. And they brought unto him a penny. And he saith unto them, Whose is this image and superscription? They say unto him, Caesar's. Then saith he unto them, 'Render therefore unto Caesar the things which are Caesar's'.

The answer is complete, and the reproof final and crushing. Nothing needs to be added. Indeed, without ruining the point, nothing *can* be added. Unfortunately, an officious busybody, one of many who have left their traces on the text of the Gospels, thought that an antithesis was needed, and attached the words, 'and unto God the things that are God's,' producing bad sense and bad theology, and giving us the false, mutually exclusive contrast of, 'the things of Caesar' and 'the things of God'. As the narrative is almost identical in all three synoptic Gospels, the interpolation was already present in the source of Mark, from whom Matthew and Luke took the passage; but that is nothing unique!

You may perhaps think that I have made a curious sort of beginning to three addresses in which a politican comments on what he thinks about the Church and the work of the world. But is it so strange? That was just where Malcolm Muggeridge and I ran slap into one of the best known of the injunctions attributed to Jesus, only to find that on investigation it turns out to be something quite different: so far from Christ distinguishing between duty to Caesar and duty to God, he said nothing of the sort. He replied, in effect, 'let Caesar answer for his own'.

The Christian Church is the church of a book. Like the Muslims, the Christians are *ahl-i-kitab*, 'people of a book'. But what a book it is! Unlike the Qur'an, in which, throughout all its history, there literally have been no variant readings whatsoever, the New Testament is the end-product of textual and historical processes of fantastic and even unfathomable complexity. No other document has come into our hands from the Greco-Roman world which approaches the Gospels in this respect; the Homeric poems, for instance, are child's play in comparison.

The Christian Church, however, is not only the church of a book. It is also the church of a rite, and that rite is mysteriously and wonderfully intertwined with the book, so that the life of each is derived from the life of the other.

Such a definition as I have just given, so briefly as not to exceed two sentences, with the intimation that I mean to say something in this section about the book and in section

II about the rite, may well provoke in more insistent form the very objection which I purported to be answering: 'How come you, instead of talking to us about Christianity in politics and Christianity in the workaday world, presume to lecture us on textual criticism and anthropology? "Who made thee ... a judge over us?" (Exod. 2.14)'.

I humbly reply in the first place, that a man can hardly say what he believes about the Church and the world without telling you what he believes about the Church. Indeed, when he has told that, he may turn out to have told all the rest, or nearly all. It always seems to me, too, much more presumption in a layman to discourse upon the relevance and application of the Church's doctrine than upon the Church itself. I am an inveterate believer in the rule *ne sutor ultra crepidam*, 'the shoemaker to his last,' and to me a priest and a layman, like a king and a subject in the famous saying of Charles I, 'are two things'. But which is the last of the shoemaker? The priest, besides an office which no layman can perform, has a pastoral duty for which, like the rest of us in our several callings, he is trained and practised, and of which not the least part is just the exposition and the mediation of that meeting between the Church and the world. But neither textual criticism, nor Greek, nor history, nor anthropology, nor, for that matter, theology, are specially the business of the clergy as clergy; and on this ground at least the layman, as layman, is no intruder.

The book and the rite of the Church demand of us, besides much else, the most intense intellectual effort of which our abilities and our knowledge render us capable, and a man's particular mental gifts and habit will determine the form which that intellectual effort most readily takes. It so happens that a strong native inclination to the textual study and criticism of written documents is something with which I came into the world and which I could not help but cultivate and cannot help but practise. It cannot be something which I leave outside the church door or switch off when I hear or read the Gospels; and of this I am sure, that we are not required by our religion to deny what our intellect takes for truth. No doubt we are required to add from other sources to that truth; but it would be a kind of blasphemy to suppose that we are ever called upon to deny it. Of all places a man needs least to argue this in an Anglican church; for it has always been one of the special features of the Church of England that it tolerated, welcomed and honoured the work of the intellect. It is a Church which has characteristically fostered scholarship and study, and its love of learning is one of the virtues which it may plead in extenuation of its deficiencies.

I will go further and say that not infrequently those who claim to eliminate all intermediate effort and go straight to the application of the Church to the world are in reality proceeding, even if not conscious of doing so, in the opposite direction: they are starting with their own opinions, wills and predispositions, and presuming to cloak them with the authority and the holiness of the Church. It is a fault not less found among the clergy than the laity, and perhaps not new but very old. I imagine it must have been very prevalent in the fourth century, when the persecuted Church became the imperial established faith. So we ought not to be ashamed to return, ever and again, to the book of the Church, with whatever of light is given to us.

One thing we know about those for whom each of the four Gospels was intended. Whoever they were, they were uninquisitive about the Ascension, which was something either indifferent and uninteresting or quite unknown to the Churches which received and used the Gospels that we have. In Matthew and John it appears not at all; in Mark and Luke it receives a perfunctory and almost embarrassed mention. The central truth and assertion of the Christian Church, the victory of Christ over death and his resurrection, whatever it meant to those for whom the Gospels were written and edited, did not imperatively necessitate the dramatic stage-machinery of the ascension. A narrative which ended without it was not for them incomplete.

The story of the journey to Emmaus is found in full only in the Gospel according to St Luke (24.13–35); but the brief mention in Mark 16.12 ('he appeared in another form unto two of them as they walked and went into the country')

implies the full narrative, which is thus cursorily sum-
marized.[1] The story is endlessly significant. Unrecognized,
the risen Christ joins two of his disciples as they travel. He
induces them to tell him the account of the ministry, the
crucifixion and the empty tomb; and then he proceeds to
demonstrate to them that the Messianic prophesies have
thereby been fulfilled. There follows the moment at the
entrance to Emmaus, from which the immortal words, 'abide
with us' have echoed round the world and through the
centuries. The point to which the entire narrative leads up is
the breaking of the bread: the stranger re-enacts the action
of the Last Supper, blessing, breaking and distributing, and
in that instant is both recognized and becomes invisible.
Whatever is the innermost secret of the event which trans-
formed human history in the principate of Tiberius Caesar,
we are so near to it in that room at the inn at Emmaus that
one almost feels its physical presence, like that of some
living person hidden only by a thin partition. I shall return
in section II to Emmaus and to the revelation which the two
travellers announced to the other disciples, that 'he was
known of them in the breaking of the bread'. For the
moment, I want to extract from the narrative, which bespeaks
a power of dramatic composition of the highest order, one
sentence only: 'We trusted,' said the two disciples to the
stranger, 'that it had been he which should have redeemed
Israel'.

Unexpectedly I have come back to the tribute money and,
'the things which are Caesar's'; but inevitably so, because
wherever one strikes a finger on the book, there the same
announcement is being made. The deliverance of Israel is
not of this world: it is a denial and a repudiation and a
contradiction of this world. From the temptation in the
wilderness to the death on the Cross this is asserted over and
over again, and we only fail to hear it whenever we cannot
bear to hear it. 'Master,' says the rich young man, 'what
good thing shall I do to have everlasting life?' And the end
of the dialogue is the command: 'Sell that thou hast and

---

[1] I now think it more probable that the words in Mark are an addition,
derived from knowledge of Luke.

give to the poor, and thou shalt have treasure in heaven, and come and follow me' (Matt. 19.16).

We would fain cling to the words, 'give to the poor', as though the command were an injunction to subscribe to charity. But that clause belongs with the one before it and simply means, 'liquidate your assets and get rid of the cash which they realise'; for merely to sell the possessions would leave the owner as well off as before. In a debate which I had in the correspondence columns of *The Times* with the Bishop of Carlisle (28/30 November 1970), the Bishop significantly paraphrased the command, 'he was bidden' (he wrote) 'to compare his material situation with that of others and to do something practical about it'. With great respect, Jesus said nothing of the kind; the paraphrase could not be further from the original. The command was a command to be divested of all possessions.

Alternatively we try to pretend that this was specifically prescribed for the rich and does not mean us; but in that case we might as well disregard the central injunction, 'do this,' on the ground that it was addressed only to the twelve.

The command, in fine, is both universal and impracticable: it is of another world. 'If any man will come after me, let him deny himself and take up his cross[2] and follow me. For whosoever will save his life shall lose it, and whosoever will lose his life for my sake, shall find it' (Matt. 16.24). This was the text which Matthew and Luke found in Mark; but it was too strong for somebody after them, whose reluctance we now trace in Mark (8.35), where after the words, 'for my sake' are interpolated the words, 'and for the Gospel'.[3] One sympathizes with that anonymous interpolator; but he knew, and we know, that this has nothing to do with missionaries in the South Sea Islands. The command is absolute, and is directed to everybody, and means what it says.

---

[2] The word *stauros*, 'cross', is grotesque here. Mark 6.8 shows that the original was *rhabdos*, 'staff', which was displaced by a theological gloss.

[3] The words 'for my sake' themselves appear to be an earlier interpolation in Mark or in his source.

The characteristic of the great mass of teaching which has been embodied in the Gospels, though different strands and elements are distinguishable, is its absolute nature. It was typical of the commandments of Judaism that, however hard and exacting, they were not impracticable. The teacher of the Gospels had deliberately rendered them impracticable (Matt. 5.27): 'Ye have heard that it was said by them of old time (that is, in the Decalogue), "Thou shalt not commit adultery"; but I say unto you that whosoever looketh on a woman to lust after her hath committed adultery with her already in his heart.' Or again: 'Ye have heard that it hath been said, "An eye for an eye, and a tooth for a tooth"; but I say unto you that ye resist not evil, but whosoever shall smite thee on thy right cheek, turn to him the other also'.

Such is the significance of that extraordinary collocation of two passages, drawn from separate books of the Pentateuch and combined together, with which we are familiar as an alternative to the Decalogue at Holy Communion. It occurs in two passages in the Gospels (Matt. 22.37; Luke 10.27), where Jesus links together the absolute command, to love the Lord Thy God, 'with all thy heart' etc., and the equally absolute command to 'love thy neighbour as thyself'. It is the absoluteness of the two commands that gives them their connection and correspondence, which they do not have in their remotely separated original contexts; and they have a remarkable textual history. The act of combining them was antecedent to their position in the Gospel narrative; for in Matthew they are the reply—and an inappropriate one, too—to the lawyer who asked what is 'the greatest commandment', while in Luke they are the reply to the question (a doublet of the passage about the rich young man, which I have already quoted): 'What shall I do to inherit eternal life?' Much more remarkable, the second commandment, 'to love thy neighbour as thyself,' has that absolute and unattainable significance not in the Hebrew original of the Pentateuch but only in the Greek translation, the so-called Septuagint,[4] which was in use and circulation in Palestine at the beginning of our era.

It is such an observation as this which affords us a glimpse into the depths which lie behind and beneath the book of the Church, as it becomes visible as a whole in the third and fourth centuries. We find a narrative, into which is woven an interpretation of the law and the prophets of Israel that removes them out of this world into a new dimension. We find the description of an event by which 'the redemption of Israel' was effected in terms of that new dimension. We find that redemption projected beyond the time of that event and the limits of Israel by an insight which dawned somehow, suddenly and irresistibly, upon a little group of men. At every point in the book the labour of the intellect penetrates further and further without ever reaching final satisfaction. In the concluding stanzas of Goethe's *Faust* the choir of angels sings of heaven as the region 'where the impossible becomes reality'. It is where he that loses his life saves it, where he that negates himself inherits everlasting life, and where the 'redemption of Israel' is recognized in the breaking of the bread; for the Church of the book is also the Church of the rite.

II

I must ask understanding for the predicament of a politician who is to say what he understands of the Church and the work of the world, and who finds that he must first try to say what he understands of the Church. He cannot escape from this necessity by alleging—what is neither logical nor true—that the Church in itself is a business for the experts (whoever they are) but the Church in relation to the world is a topic open to amateurs. On the contrary, if it be presumption to discourse upon the Church, still more is it presumption to expatiate about what the Church has to say

[4] Lev. 19, 18 and Deut. 6, 5. The Hebrew means 'love thy neighbour, (seeing he is) as thou (art)', cf. Lev. 19, 34 (see E. Ullendorf, in *Studies in Memory of Leon Roth*, 1966, 273ff.), whereas the Greek unambiguously means 'as (thou lovest) thyself'.

to the world; for this must be the profounder and more perilous task. 'Woman, what have I to do with thee?' (John 2.4) was the strange preface to, 'that first miracle which he did in Cana of Galilee'. That we commonly suppose otherwise, is only a sign of our readiness to claim the sanction and authority of the Church for what happen to be our own wishes or prejudices.

In the previous section I described the Christian church as being the Church of a book and the Church of a rite; and it was of the book that I spoke. In this section therefore I must speak of the rite.

In the ducal palace at Urbino in Tuscany, that wonderful Renaissance creation of Federigo da Montefeltro, there is a picture of the Last Supper by Justus van Ghent. It shows Christ and the disciples, with a strange fringe of spectators, including the Duke himself and the Persian ambassador. But this is no ordinary Last Supper. It is not the scene of Christ sitting at table with the twelve, as we are familiar with it in countless variations upon the theme which Leonardo da Vinci made unforgettable. In this picture the disciples are kneeling, and Christ, who stands, is distributing to them wafers from a paten, exactly as the priest administers the sacrament. We know what words accompany the action in the picture: 'This is my body'. The painter has put before us in visual form a haunting commentary upon the world's most unfathomable sentence. There are minor variants, as well as additions, to that sentence in the three synoptic Gospels (Matt. 26.26; Mark 14.22; Luke 22.19)— the event itself is not in the Gospel according to St John at all—and in that other witness, the first Pauline epistle to the Corinthians (11.24); but those words, and those alone, are common to all: 'This is my body'.

In the Gospel narrative of the Last Supper Christ pronounces these words before Gethsemane, the trial and the crucifixion; but the picture at Urbino says something about them which we scarcely dare to think, let alone to say: they can only be pronounced by a supernatural Christ; for only if his historical body is not present, can it be true, or even conceivable, that he can predicate of the bread: 'This is

my body'. Otherwise the collision in time is not merely
unimaginable; it is grotesque. The Christ who says: 'This
is my body' is the Christ of the inn at Emmaus, the unrecognized stranger, the risen Christ, who, at the moment when
he brake the bread and gave it to the two disciples there,
'was known of them and vanished'. It is the fact which the
Eastern Church recognizes by acknowledging the host rather
as the risen body of Christ than, like the Western Church, as
the slain victim. It is the fact which is thrust upon us by the
exigencies of translation out of Greek. In Greek the present
tense is also used for the future. So, in the words which have
entered our liturgies from an interpolation in later manu-
scripts of the Gospel according to St Luke only, the Greek
present participle passive, which our Book of Common
Prayer translates as, 'which is given for you', leaves the
riddle of time unsolved: is it present? is it future? Nor does
St Paul help us; for in the earliest text of Corinthians there
is no verb at all: 'This is my body, for you'. Translation
is forced to cut the knot. Our English version does it one
way, 'which *is* given for you'; it is present. The vernacular
Roman Mass cuts the knot the other way, 'which *will be*
given up for you': it is future.

I suppose the most powerful intellectual experience of my
boyhood was the encounter with J. G. Frazer's *Golden
Bough*. Far beyond any other influence, it set me adrift from
the Church in which I had been confirmed, to wander for
many a year before I could return 'to my father's house'.
Here, beyond all doubt, was the evidence of a widespread,
if not universal, human mode of behaviour: the apparently
irresistible necessity to kill God and eat him, and the
accompanying belief that survival, in this physical world
and in another, spirit world, could only be ensured by doing
just that thing. That Christ is the God-king, who is slain,
eaten and renewed, and thereby enables his subjects and
worshippers to triumph with him over natural death, this
was only too evident. That the God who says; 'This is my
body' is the corn spirit, and that the God who says: 'This
is my body' is the vine spirit, and that both these, who date
from the recent, agricultural period of mankind, had a long

line of predecessors in the dark predatory period of man's history—this also was only too evident. Christ, Christianity and the Church had crumbled and vanished; or rather, they were now dried and labelled specimens in a large case in the museum of anthropology. They had been explained; and now they could be explained away. Into the chamber 'swept and garnished' by J. G. Frazer I was ready to welcome the master of the 'clean sweep' (*reinen Tisch machen*), Zarathustra Nietzsche, who brought the news that, 'God is dead; he has died of his compassion for humanity'.

I have already expressed my conviction that it can by no means be required of us to deny what our intellect takes for truth, whatever of additional truth we may obtain from elsewhere; and I do not believe that we are required to refuse the unmistakable evidence that there is a link between the risen Christ who says: 'This is my body' and the priest-victim-kings whom mankind has worshipped and eaten from time immemorial. The resemblances are not accident, cannot be accident. The rite of the Church embodies a theme of primeval antiquity, and the book of the Church is to that theme as the words of a song are to the music. The error is to conclude that this fact invalidates either the rite or the book. On the contrary, there is a sense in which they could not be valid without it.

It is ironical that in the nineteenth century the discovery and exploration of the process of evolution were supposed to be inimical to Christianity and destructive of it. Disraeli's famous Oxford joke about being 'on the side of the angels' —as against all that was identified with Darwin—was exactly one hundred and eighty degrees out. As our understanding, or at any rate our inkling, of the origin and survival of humanity deepens, we find that two, superficially contradictory, aspects of the Church which presented severe difficulty to pre-evolutionary thinking become intelligible and even indispensable. One of these aspects is the historical uniqueness of its origin; the other is its manifest growth out of previous human religious experience and behaviour.

The Christian Church asserts, as its central fact, an event in history, in a way that perhaps no other does. The only evidence for what that event was is the Church itself, its rite and its book. Indeed, the event is unknowable outside the Church. Whoever wrote the celebrated interpolation in Josephus was as misguided as the indefatigable Empress Helena, whose explorations enjoyed the sort of success which royal archaeologists tend to encounter with suspicious regularity. Nevertheless, something happened at a particular point of time which not only changed human history but which was so important that the difference between knowing and not knowing it, believing it and not believing it, could not be described in terms less stark than the difference between life and death. This was something which both the reason and the moral conscience of pre-Darwinian man (if I may allow myself that shorthand expression) found intolerably difficult of digestion, and an account of the endeavours which have been made to escape from the Gospel's combination of being both unique and historical would occupy volumes. For post-Darwinian man there is no puzzle at all. He knows that suddenness and uniqueness is the normal character of the events by which the story of mankind and of his universe is rendered intelligible. Something happened which had never happened before, and after which everything else was bound to be different: the account of what we call evolution is punctuated by that form of statement. It is not abnormal; it is the norm. If anything important was going to occur, we would expect it to be both sudden and unique.

At the same time we have moved beyond the notion of the evolution of the species as the explanation of the characteristics of individual specimens to the idea of the evolution of societies as the explanation of behaviour. Therefore the 'survival of the fittest' has been placed in a new context. We have at least begun to suspect that the emotional and intellectual experience of mankind and the patterns of behaviour of men in society have a function as important as their physiological characteristics, but far more subtle and inaccessible. Man's myths have played as much part in man's evolution and survival as his fingers and his buttocks. For instance, the beliefs and practices which can be analysed and classified under the heading of sympathetic magic, and attributed, as Frazer attributed them, to errors of reasoning, like the logical fallacy that 'like causes like', may in reality have a much deeper cause and serve a necessary function. In that case, it would be surprising, in fact unintelligible, if these patterns of thought and behaviour were any less persistent than the other products of man's evolution. That the rite and the myth of the Church grow out of earlier religious experience would be predictable, and would have been essential to its initial victory and its subsequent survival.

This combination of uniqueness and repetitiveness is at the heart of the rite of the Church, and defies or punishes every attempt to resolve it by banishing one aspect or the other. They exist in it side by side, as two aspects of the same thing, and in attempting to tear them apart Christendom has only torn itself apart. 'A full, perfect and sufficient sacrifice, oblation and satisfaction ... of himself once offered'; that is the defiant assertion of the historically unique, only to be followed by the present drama (or action) of the priest-victim-conqueror and the words, which mean nothing unless they mean everything: 'This is my body', the words which the Church has said since the Church was.

On the road to Emmaus (Luke 24.13–35) the unrecognized risen Christ explained to the two disciples who 'trusted that it had been he which should have redeemed Israel,' that this had indeed happened; but they did not understand. Only when he performed the rite were 'their eyes opened and they knew him' and only after that did they understand what he had been saying. 'And they said one to another. Did not our heart burn within us while he talked with us by the way and while he opened to us the scriptures?' The redemption of Israel had been given a wholly new sense, lifted out of one dimension into another, out of one world into another; and the agency by which this was comprehended was a parallel transformation of the immemorial, and perhaps indispensable, act of eating God. The sublimation of the primeval form of thought and observance was itself a revelation of the new truth that 'he that findeth his life shall lose it, and he that loseth his life for my sake shall find it' (Matt. 10.39).

The words are a self-contradiction, and are intended to be so. It is part of the impossibility which lies at the heart of the assertions and the commands of Christ and which is reflected in the impossibility of the historical but continuing action of self-giving.

The pagan and hostile neighbours of the early Church could not believe that it was bread and wine of which the Christians partook in their mysterious rite, prepared for by so much instruction and initiation. It must, at the very least, they thought, be human sacrifice. Rumour and malice, the fomentors of persecution, asserted that the Christians stole babies and killed them in order to eat the flesh and drink the blood. It was impossible that in the central and culminating act of the new faith there should be the simplest and commonest of objects and the simplest and most incomprehensible of statements. If they had been in Pontius Pilate's judgement hall they would have heard Christ's words, though they would not have understood them: 'My kingdom is not of this world' (John 18.36). And they would have heard the answer of the priests: 'We have no king but Caesar' (John 19.15).

III

I only noticed afterwards that in each of the two previous sections I had described the beginning of the Church as, 'an event which changed the course of human history'. Perhaps I wrote those words more instinctively than deliberately. Yet they were not a flourish of the pen, and I would not wish to unwrite them. But in what sense are they true? It might, or might not, be possible to prove—I very much doubt it—that the manner in which the two Roman Empires, of the West and of the East, gave place to an utterly new organization of the inhabitants of southern and western Europe and of the Mediterranean basin was conditioned by the Church and its consequences. There

might be more chance of proving that the culture of Europe
—with its later influence on the rest of the world—would
have been very different if the inheritance of the Greco-
Roman Age had descended through channels which did not
include the Church and Christianity. Yet it was certainly
none of this that I meant.

Still less could I have meant that mankind has been
decisively better, or even better at all, in any sense of the
word not specially chosen for the purpose of yielding the
desired answer. If the object of the operation had been 'to
make us good', it would have to be written off as an unquali-
fied failure. Special pleading can select features of modern
Christendom, such as the absence of slavery or the progressive disappearance of brutal punishments, and compare it
favourably in those respects with the non-Christian world
or with the Greco-Roman civilization; but it is necessary
then to ignore features of Christendom, medieval and
modern, which by any standard are as savage and repulsive
as human annals know. In any case, there is the fatal fact
that even the selected favourable symptoms do not (to put
it mildly) coincide with any increase in the sway or influence
of the Church.

I ended the last section with the words of Christ to Pontius
Pilate: 'My Kingdom is not of this world'. That Kingdom
is the 'thy Kingdom' of the Lord's Prayer. The eleventh
canto of Dante's *Purgatory* opens with one of the most
marvellous passages in even that marvellous work. The laden
spirits, whose sin to be expiated was pride, recite the Lord's
Prayer. Dante has turned it into those Italian triplets, *terza
rima*, of which the whole vast work consists, making each
verse of the Prayer the first line of the triplet, and following
it with two lines of commentary. As well as I can render it,
'Thy Kingdom come' runs as follows: 'Come unto us thy
Kingdom and thy peace; for if it come not unto us, hard
though we toil, we can not thither tend'.

Our own minds, even in this last third of the twentieth
century, are so saturated with the notions of progress and
improvement that statements such as those are not merely
repudiated, but bounce off before we can even take them in.

Our whole lives and vocabulary, down to the percentage of economic 'growth' which we compare from month to month, because even a year seems too long to wait for seeing some improvement, are lived in an assumed state of progression. It was easier for Christians of those many centuries before progress had been invented. To say that they saw the world as static is a misconception. Change was as much the environment of their lives as of ours; but it was not interpreted in terms of progression or (what is the same thing the other way round) retrogression: their contact was between God 'who changeth not' and a world of change, but not a world of progress. To be presented with the idea of a kingdom which is not only not of this world but which comes to us, not we to it, is about as bleak an affront as could be imagined by minds full of the idea of self-generated progress. No doubt the idea of progress—I will be crude, and say 'improvement'—is one of the articles which must be left outside that entrance through which, according to one of the hardest and most impossible of the sayings (Matt. 18.3; 19.14), only 'children' or those, 'as children', may pass.

There is another gateway through which luggage, physical as well as mental, is not allowed to be taken. We may construct what fantasies we please about society; but the individual is born once, lives once, and dies once; and it is to him that the Kingdom, if it comes at all, comes. Perhaps that is the most offensive fact of all to an age where everything is social or collective—that the Gospel and the action of the Church is to individuals, and only to individuals, and that the Kingdom and the everlasting life of which the Church speaks and which Christ promises are to individuals. From the slave or the patrician or the emperor in the Greco-Roman world to the 'man in the pew' in the City church or the peasant in the Polish village, there is no progression, no moving forward or back; they are all, to whom the bread is given, 'children'. If they form a community, it is of individuals who have this thing in common; if they form a body, it is a 'mystical body', which (being translated) means the body of initiates, of those who have entered the same gateway; it is a community, like the Kingdom, 'not of this world'.

When the Socrates of Plato was asked what justice is, as Pilate once asked, 'what is truth?'—incidentally, I doubt if Francis Bacon was right in supposing that Pilate was 'jesting' —he said: first of all I must elicit a just community, and then, as a member of that community, I will show you a just man, and be able to tell you what justice is. That was very Greek, that was very compelling—you will hear plenty of people saying today that they can only be good in a good society—but it is not the way of the Church. That is the 'redemption of Israel' in the sense in which Christ rejected it; call it reform, or call it revolution, or call it, within the Roman empire, rebellion. The Gospel is not a social gospel; it is not a gospel about society. The Gospel is not the *Republic* of Plato; it is the opposite pole to the *Republic* of Plato, because it is to individuals and announced a Kingdom not of this world, which comes to men and not from men.

'Mr Powell, we knew that politicians were notorious for not answering the question; but you have carried prevarication beyond a joke. Here are we patiently waiting, and now we are half-way through your third piece, and still you will not tell us how, in the work of the world—in your life as a politician or ours in the City—the Church causes us or helps us or commands us to do differently from what we would otherwise do.' Certainly I have not answered that question, save to say, by implication—and now, if you like, explicitly—that I believe there is no more answer to it than Christ gave about the tribute money, which was a repudiation of the very question. I do not believe I can go to the Church and ask it to give me answers to the great questions of my political life; and if I imagine that I am getting them, I am self-deceived and deaf to what the Church *is* saying to me. 'And a certain politician, seeking guidance, asked him, Is it lawful for the United Kingdom to accede to the European Economic Community?' Imagine the scorn with which Christ would have responded to such an inquiry. 'What', he would have asked, '*is* the United Kingdom, and what have I to do with it? My Kingdom is not of this world.' But as a politician I have everything to do with the United Kingdom, as the banker has to do with deposits and credits, and the potter with pots.

When I busy myself with the social services or economic growth, what I get by way of answer is the Sermon on the Mount (Matt. 5.3ff.; Luke 6.20ff.): 'Blessed are they which do hunger and thirst' and 'Blessed are the poor'. People like to talk about the Sermon on the Mount, but they do not like to listen to what it says. They never have done, not since the days of the interpolator in Matthew, who said to himself: 'Come, come, this will never do,' and slipped in the words, 'hunger and thirst *after righteousness*' and 'poor *in spirit*', to make Christ's words harmless and smug. But Christ did not say that; he said that it is better to be hungry than well-fed; that it is better to be poor than rich. All the objects of your lives and mine, all the worthy aspirations and achievements which will deserve an honoured and comfortable old age, a knighthood or the Queen's Award for Industry, a favourable mention in the history books—or maybe the fame of a Marlborough or a Churchill—they are not just nothing, says the Church; they are less than nothing. With these you cannot come in; with these you cannot enter through the eye of the needle. All those distinctions and differences without which the life of the world is unimaginable, however the world handles them—it is not so much that Christ has abolished them—in Christ they do not exist: 'There is neither Jew nor Greek, there is neither bond nor free, there is neither male nor female' (Gal. 3.28).

So we fall back upon individual morality, and try to reassure ourselves that though Christ and the Church have no instructions to give to the world in which men and women live, they have instructions for the men and women themselves; but only to be confronted by the same response. The Church does not, for instance, enjoin upon you honesty in worldly getting, nor upon me benevolence in parliamentary legislating. 'After all these things do the Gentiles seek' (Matt. 6.32); they have as little to do with the Church as keeping to the left or giving way at major roads. The com-

mand of the Church to men and women is to have nothing
to do with the world, 'to keep themselves unspotted from it'
(James 1.27). And if I am told that it is not fair to quote
pastoral epistles, because those were only intended for the
primitive churches, tiny, obscure groups in a pagan world,
then I will go straight to the absolute and anti-social nature
of the central command of Christ and the Church, that ye
love one another even as I have loved you, that we love our
neighbour as ourselves, that we are all one body because we
all partake of the one bread. It was quite deliberately that
I used the adjective 'anti-social' of this command, because
no human society can comply with it—and that, not in the
sense that it is an ideal, unattainable perhaps, but one to
which societies can more or less approximate, but in the
sense that it is destructive of, and incompatible with, any
conceivable society. Indeed, the use of the word 'ideal' is
yet another pair of dark glasses with which we protect
ourselves from looking straight into what Christ and the
Church say. The emperor Julian the apostate was perfectly
right when he affirmed that, if Jesus' precepts were to be
followed, no city, no nation, no house could endure.

'As in Adam all die, even so in Christ shall all be made
alive' (1 Cor. 15.22). This is a statement which has become
intelligible again to post-Darwinian man. Indeed, to post-
Darwinian man the whole doctrine of the fall and original
sin has become more than intelligible; it has become compelling. The arrival of self-consciousness in the world through
humanity started a train which does not contain its own
ending and created problems which do not contain their own
solution. The work of Christ is not the improvement or
perfecting of the process which started, in Biblical metaphor,
with Adam. On the contrary, it is a repudiation of it, and
the being made alive in Christ is the denial and undoing of
what is inseparable from Adam, both individually and in
society; for Adam is a social animal, known and knowable
only as such. St Paul rendered this intelligible to himself in
his own terms of the Jewish law and its supersession. We
may render it intelligible to ourselves in terms of biology
and anthropology. But the outcome is the same : the morality

of the Gospel, like the Kingdom of heaven, is 'not of this world'.

We have run ourselves into an old, old dilemma. We are left with the world and the Church, and no bridge between the two, but rather a logical gulf, on the absoluteness of which we are driven to insist upon pain of denying what is essential Christianity. We shall find no resolution therefore in logic; for no resolution exists; the irreconcilable live side by side in human nature. The dilemma is of the nature of humanity and, in a special sense, of the nature of Christendom.

When the hearers grew impatient with the preacher (Eccles. 12.13), as you, with all the work of the world to be done, are no doubt long since impatient with me, they cried out: 'Let us hear the conclusion of the whole matter'; but they were sent away with an answer that they knew before they came: 'Fear God and keep his commandments; for this is the whole duty of man'. That *was* the answer, before the event which changed the course of human history; but that event, you will remember, was 'unto the Jews a stumbling block, and unto the Greeks foolishness' (1 Cor. 1.23). It could not be contained within the morality of the commandments, nor comprehended within the terms of the intellect. Otherwise it could not have spanned the gulf in human nature and reconciled its irreconcilables, with the assertion: 'I have overcome the world' (John 16.33), and the action: 'This is my body'.

8

NOT OF THIS WORLD

Discussion of the preceding essay
with Professor Dennis Nineham

NINEHAM

Perhaps, Mr Powell, we shall best get our discussion started
if I begin by telling you my general reaction to what you
said; and I think I'd like to start by saying something about
the text from the New Testament which you used. I feel
that you've misinterpreted the passage, partly I suspect
because you began, rather surprisingly perhaps, by mis-
translating it. You know as well as I do that in the original
Greek what Jesus said to Pilate (John 18.36) was: 'My
Kingdom, or my authority, is not *out* of this world', 'out of'
in the sense of being derived from, or being based upon,
this world; and you will know as well as I do that the word
'world' in St John's Gospel has a very special, almost a
technical, meaning. It means human society organized apart
from God and indeed in opposition to the will of God. What
Jesus is here saying to Pilate is in effect: 'Yes, it's perfectly
true, I possess authority just as you do, but your authority
and the authority of other worldly rulers is based upon the
needs and the circumstances of *this* world'. For example,
Pilate owed his authority to the fact that he had been
appointed by a powerful Emperor. Some rulers owe their
authority to the fact that they've been put in power by a
political decision of the majority of their fellow citizens.
Others owe their political power to the fact that they've
been put into power and kept in power by a military junta.
But, Jesus is saying, although I have authority, it is not an
authority which is derived in any of those ways, or in any

other way, from the circumstances of *this* world; my authority comes direct from God, direct from *outside* this world. The point of what Jesus here says concerns only the force of his authority and not the sphere of its exercise. He says, 'my authority does not arise *out* of this world' but he says nothing to suggest that the world is not the sphere *in* which his authority is and ought to be exercised. You say that according to the New Testament the Kingdom of God is something which is given, which comes, and which is not brought by anything that men do or fail to do; and with that I entirely agree. The New Testament knows, as you say, nothing of automatic improvement or progress. But from the fact that nothing we do can succeed in bringing the Kingdom, nothing we do can earn or merit salvation, it doesn't follow—though people have often thought it did—that what we do is of no importance at all in relation to God. On the contrary, the New Testament throughout, it seems to me, says that anyone who has really heard the gospel of the coming of God's Kingdom and who has really believed it, who has really understood and accepted all that this amazing act of forgiveness and generosity on God's part means, will be bound to respond by showing a certain quality of life, by behaving in certain ways *here in this world*. It seems to me one of the elements that you've failed to notice is that the coming of the Kingdom is judgement. Jesus says (Matt. 7.21), 'Not everyone who says to me, "Lord, Lord" shall enter into the Kingdom of heaven, but he that does the will of my Father which is in heaven'; and then he pictures what it will be like when the Kingdom comes (Matt. 25.31ff.)— the people who get into the Kingdom are the people who've demonstrated their faith by giving cups of cold water to people who've needed them, by visiting people in prison, by feeding the hungry and so on. The test is how people have behaved in this world. Likewise St Paul (Gal. 5.21) lists a whole lot of sinful types of action and then he says: 'I tell you, as I have told you before, that they who do such things will not enter the Kingdom of heaven'. Every single New Testament writer, in one way or another—and they do it in very different ways—links faith, being a Christian, with

behaving in the world towards one's neighbour, towards
other people, both individually and corporately, in certain
ways, and avoiding behaving towards them in certain other
ways. It seems to me that it's this element, and I regard it
as an absolutely vital element, in the New Testament that
you leave out of account.

POWELL

I'm very grateful to you for the additional colour, if I may
so put it, which you've given to the words of Christ to
Pilate. Having declared, as you've explained, that his
authority in this world was not derived from the same source
as Pilate's or any other worldly authority, what did Christ
proceed to do? He proceeded, in some sense about which
we continue all our lives to reflect without fully fathoming
it, to be sacrificed. He did not proceed to exercise this
authority, derived from God the Father, in order to alter
the world. He did something which, in the vulgar phrase,
was 'out of this world'. Now I'm far from saying, and I
hope that nothing which I've said would be understood to
mean, that it is of no importance what a man does. On the
contrary, one of the aspects of Christianity seems to me to
be that it endows what we all do day by day with a kind of
awful importance. What Christianity does not do, to my
understanding, is to describe a 'will of the Father' (I'm
using the phrase which you used) from which we can
draw deductions as to political action, social organization,
all the practical choices which men make in life between
one course of action and another. The cup of water, the
visiting of the widow and the fatherless, the expression of the
sense of common humanity between one man and another—
there's still the same logically unbridgeable gulf between
these individual reactions of one person to another and
social organization or political decision.

NINEHAM

I feel that is really a half truth. You've said that the Gospel
is not a social gospel, it is not a gospel about society. In one
sense I agree: the Gospel makes no attempt to lay down
a blueprint for the way society should be run, either in its

own day or in any subsequent day. On the other hand I regard this as a half truth, because it seems to me that what the Gospel does say is that when a man becomes a Christian, his whole being, his whole attitude is changed, is assimilated to the mind of Christ in every conceivable situation and relationship in which he finds himself. It's perfectly true that in the New Testament the emphasis falls mainly on how that will work out between Christians within the Church and between Christians and non-Christians mainly on an individual level. That's mainly because the early Christians were, after all, not people of any great power or social position and therefore they weren't likely to come up against situations in which they had to exercise political judgement or political power. Nevertheless, the whole logic of the New Testament message seems to me to be that, whatever situation a Christian finds himself in, whether it be personal relationships, or whether the politician be making judgements which will affect corporate things, and exercising social and political power, all this will be affected by his position as a Christian; and if he really is a Christian, this fact will manifest itself in his behaviour in the social and political areas just as much as in any others. Indeed, I think you can already begin to feel that in the New Testament itself. St Paul, for example, tells the Romans (13.6) that they must willingly pay their taxes; or the author of 1 Timothy (2.1) urges Christians regularly to pray for the emperor and his political assistants, because it is the will of God that the Roman Empire should continue in an orderly way. The author of 1 Peter (2.13ff.) has the same thing to say. Even Jesus is reported in St Matthew's Gospel (17.24ff.) as giving an example, through Peter, of paying the Temple tax.

POWELL

I don't think those are very helpful cases, because they are cases of compliance with existing authority—for example, accepting the current tax system, justified or unjustified, whatever may be its implications or consequences. But let's bring this to a test. You say that we ought to be able to see and judge the difference between a Christian and one who is not in the way he acts in political life. Well, *I*'ve got a decision to make in the next two months: I've got to go into one lobby or the other—and before doing so, I've got to make my views and reasons clear—on the question whether this country should accede to the Treaty of Rome, to the EEC. Neither I, nor those who will vote the other way, are going to vote with any uncharitable intention towards their fellow-men or with the intention of doing harm, of making one blade grow where two blades grew before. Yet, although this is arguably one of the big dividing points in British political history, the Church and Christianity, unless one forces and wrenches and prostitutes them to one's political purpose, are, by their nature, silent. It may well be that the men who walk into either lobby will be different men, in some sense, according to whether, and according to the extent to which, they are assimilated, as you say, to the mind of Christ; but I do not see how a deduction can be drawn from the one to the other—from the faith and the life of a Christian to the political decision.

NINEHAM
You're asking for something which neither the New Testament nor the mainstream of Christian tradition has ever claimed to give. It has never, I think, claimed to give a specific and detailed answer about exceedingly complicated issues such as Britain's entry into the Common Market. But to say that is surely not to say that membership of Christ, membership of the Church, has not got a great deal to do with the way in which an individual politician, such as yourself, will and should make his decision on such questions. I suppose that a Christian will always keep before his mind the fact of God's creatorship of the world and his lordship over the world he has created. And he will, therefore, start by saying: 'Whatever the rights and wrongs of this issue, God must have a will for it. It must be his will for his world that at this moment one thing should be done rather than another. Therefore, a Christian's aim will be

to seek the will of God in this particular situation'.

POWELL
So you're telling me that there is no blueprint in the New Testament and yet that there's a will of God in this matter which I can seek somehow to ascertain and implement. If there is anything I am being told by the Church about this decision in which I have to participate, it is, it seems to me, that all this in the end is nothing—if you like, less than nothing. It is not the importance but the unimportance in the scale of realities, not merely of the decision whether Britain accedes to the Treaty of Rome, but of the status of the United Kingdom itself, of patriotism itself, of country itself. Christianity may perhaps be speaking to me about those things but once again I shall find a gulf opening at my feet between my recognition of the truth of what the Church tells me—that these are transitory, evanescent instants in the mind of God—and the actions and decisions which I have to take in practical life.

NINEHAM
I believe there is a very serious confusion there. I don't believe that either the New Testament or Jesus tell you that these things are of no importance. Just consider again Matthew, Chapter 25: the thing on which a man's fate hung when it came to entry or non-entry into the Kingdom was whether or not he had given a cup of cold water to one child who needed it. This seems to me to be absolutely vital in the mind of Jesus. From one point of view nothing might seem to be less important than this one act; but for him it's important because it shows where the person concerned stands, and this is for him the vital thing.

POWELL
Very well, now take me on from this 'cup of cold water', this act of self-declaration, of self-sacrifice, a kind of infinitely remote mirror-image of the sacrifice of the Saviour himself. Take me on from that to the decisions of practical political life, between one course of action and another; and what do you find? You find men ranged against one another

on both sides of the question with equal integrity, equal charity, equal good intent, speaking secularly. On which side is the 'cup of cold water'? Is the 'cup of cold water' on the side of joining the Common Market, or against? Please don't take refuge in saying: 'Oh, but this is very complicated'. I'll come nearer home, I'll take the Family Incomes Supplement Bill. Now, I know *you* wouldn't do so; but one can easily make a parody of this, and say: 'Well, of course, it's obvious that the "cup of cold water" is on the side of the proposed new social payment out of taxation'. You would scorn such a line of reasoning, and say, as I do, that we must look to the consequences and form a judgement, given human nature as it is, of the results of one system as opposed to another. Yet on both sides of that question we shall find men who bow, not with full comprehension but with a sense of compulsion, to the statement which you have repeated that the 'cup of cold water' can be the difference between surviving and not surviving, between being saved and being lost. So I still find the gulf before me.

NINEHAM
Yes, but haven't Christians realized for centuries that their religion gives them no immediate, easy, ready-made answers to the political and social, or indeed very often to the private moral questions, that they are brought up against? But why is this surprising, why is it particularly illuminating? Why does it seem to you something that you feel you want to ram home to us?

POWELL
It seemed to me worth saying, since it appears to be so widely assumed that deductions as to personal, and certainly as to political, action and as to social organization and behaviour *can* be drawn from the doctrine of the Church. I was however trying to say more than that. I was trying to convey something positive as to what I felt of the content of what the Church and Christ give to the members of the Church and to the members of Christ. Yet it did seem

even on the negative side to be a critique or criticism worth offering.

NINEHAM
Well I personally, as you will see, have considerable sympathy with *some* of the things you are saying. Indeed, I daresay in certain respects I should go further than you because I don't believe that you can ever 'read off' Christian answers from the New Testament or any other source. But you seem to go to the opposite extreme and imply, at any rate, that a man's Christian discipleship will have no effects whatsoever upon the way that he acts politically or the decisions that he takes. It doesn't seem to me that from the true things that you have said this totally negative conclusion even *begins* to follow; and it appears to me wholly contrary to the mind and statements both of the New Testament and indeed of the Christian Church.

POWELL
Perhaps we might be able to agree at any rate on this. Certainly there will be a difference—if there were not, what would we be talking about?—and indeed a fundamental difference, between the behaviour and the life of such a man and of another; but it would be a difference which you or I or anyone else might well not be able to perceive, which might well escape our own or any human judgement.

9

THAT CUP OF COLD WATER

There occurs in St Matthew (25.31ff.)—and only in St Matthew—a passage greatly beloved by the devotees of the 'social gospel'. It is the last of a series of parables and say-ings—they include the Wise and Foolish Virgins—concerned with the Last Judgement. It begins: 'When the Son of Man shall come in his glory and all the angels with him, then he shall sit on the throne of his glory and all the nations shall be brought together before him'. The King separates them to his right and left, as a shepherd separates the sheep from the goats. Then he says to those on the right: 'Come hither, ye blessed of my Father, inherit the Kingdom prepared for you from the foundation of the world'; and there follow the famous words: 'For I was hungry and ye gave me to eat,' etc. Those thus addressed, now described as 'the just', reply, 'Lord, when saw we thee hungry', etc? and receive the reply: 'Verily I say unto you, inasmuch as ye did it to one of these my brethren, the least ones, ye did it to me'. There follows a mirror image on the left, ending, 'inasmuch as ye did it not to one of these the least ones, ye did it not to me'.

It is one of those passages which seem exceedingly simple until they are read carefully. As soon however as we try to understand the scene, we are in difficulties, which are only resolved when it is observed that two distinct—and con-tradictory—elements have been combined. One is a perfectly straightforward 'doom': the blest are separated from the damned, and both are despatched to the places predestined for them respectively. Into this picture has been introduced a different one, which depicts the reward or punishment of those who have been kind or unkind, respectively, to a third group, designated as 'these, my brethren, the least ones'.

There is no place in the 'doom' for this third contingent. Surely they too must have been in the ranks of the blest. They cannot, one feels, be among the damned! Yet they are treated as entirely separate from both the blest and the damned, though these together evidently make up the whole of humanity.

The two pictures have different 'morals' and belong to different orders of thought: the first is severely fatalist, the second is cautionary. From what context the second picture comes is apparent when we inquire who these people are who are called 'the least' and with whom the King identifies himself to the point of rewarding or punishing eternally those who treated them well or ill.

What the King does not say is what he is commonly misheard as saying, namely, 'wherever anyone is hungry, or thirsty, or naked etc., that person is I'. It is not indiscriminate benevolence, but discrimination in benevolence, which is rewarded. There is no doubt about the sense in which the term 'the least ones' is used. It does not, and cannot, mean the wretched. The best commentary on it is in a saying which appears both in Matthew (10.42) and in Mark (9.41):

MATTHEW

Whoever gives one of these little ones a cup of cold water only, in the quality of a disciple, verily I say unto you, he shall not lose his reward.

MARK

Whoever gives you a cup of water, in the quality that (or, because) ye are Christ's, verily I say unto you that he shall not lose his reward.

Through the positive hailstorm of notes and explanations which have forced their way into the text, the equations are clear. 'Little ones' equals 'disciples' equals 'Christ's own'. Both passages go back to an original which said in advance what the King says in retrospect: 'Whoever gives these little ones a cup of cold water shall be rewarded'. In the course of editing,[1] 'little ones' was replaced by 'you' (addressing

---

[1] The editing includes the substitution of 'water' in Mark for Matthew's word 'cold' (*psychron*), which in itself means 'cold water'.

the disciples); to make assurance doubly sure, the words, 'in the quality of a disciple' were inserted; and, as ill luck would have it, an interlinear note, 'because ye are Christ's,' not only got into the text but displaced the words, 'of a disciple', producing the awkward combination, 'in the quality because ye are Christ's'.

In case there were any doubt about the matter, there are similar sayings in the same collection, such as, 'he that taketh you in, taketh in me' (Matt. 10.40), or 'whosoever offendeth one of these little ones, the believers on me, it were better for him that a millstone were hung round his neck and he were cast into the sea' (Mark 9.42; Matt. 18.6). In fact, 'little ones' or 'least ones' was simply the term—used in the inner circle—for believers, disciples; in short, for Christians.

The message in all these passages is spelt out at great length in the secondary strand of the description of the Last Judgement, which, with its tedious mirror image, repeating for the damned the reverse of what was said to the blest, reads like an elaboration of the cup-of-cold-water saying. The message is that in the long run it will pay to be kind to Christ's followers and will be disastrous to be beastly to them. This was no doubt an encouragement or consolation to a small persecuted minority; but it has as little to do with a gospel of general benevolence and charity as the passage about the millstone has to do with being kind to children.

10

POLITICS AND PROFESSION

Dialogue with Joseph McCulloch[1]

McCULLOCH

Mr Powell, of the many letters I have had recently most
have asked me to raise the topic of the Christian profession
and the problems that politicians have obviously to face and
the reconciliation that they have to make between their
Christian ideals and what can be done. I'd like to begin
on that at once by asking you, if I may, how *you* deal with
the problem (which we all have to deal with whether we
are politicians or not) of our Christian profession and what
we have to do in our existing situations.

POWELL

I find it—I confess at once—a dilemma, indeed, an insoluble
dilemma. I suspect that it is intended to be insoluble, and
that if I found an easy solution to it—perhaps I shall find
one at last—I would probably be misunderstanding
Christianity. I find that Christianity presents a series of
absolute commands, so complete, far-reaching and absolute,
that they are literally unfulfillable. Let me take one, which
goes straight to the heart of very much of the business of
politics, at any rate in modern times: 'Take no thought for
the morrow' (Matt. 6.34). The entire economy of the modern
state is built up by taking thought for the morrow, comparing one thought for the morrow, in terms of self-interest
or growth rate, with another thought for the morrow; and
yet I am told: 'Take no thought for the morrow'. I refuse
to be put off by the explanation: Oh, when Christ said that,

[1] St Mary-le-Bow, Cheapside, London, 21 January 1969.

he was addressing his own disciples and giving them private instruction. He was also addressing his own disciples when he said: 'Do this in remembrance of me' (Luke 22.19); and we take that to be binding upon all of us. So there straight away I am faced with an impossibility.

McCULLOCH

I'm not very happy about this because, being in the presence of a very distinguished Greek scholar, he will know that the actual Greek, translated 'take no thought' in the Authorized Version, really means, 'take no *anxious* thought for the morrow'. It means, don't be over-worried about tomorrow.

POWELL

I hardly dare say this; but that is another evasion. I realize that μέριμνα means 'anxious care'; but then a person when he invests his money takes anxious care about the prospects of profit upon it. If you take the command in its context it also says that, 'all these things will be added unto you': the provision for the morrow will be forthcoming. Yet the whole of a modern economy, indeed of any human economy, is built upon the assumption that they will not be forthcoming unless you do worry in the present. So immediately I would seem to be presented with two different worlds, and I am invited to recognize the existence of that other world. Now, perhaps, if I succeed in recognizing the existence of that other world in which those absolutes apply, I may behave differently in this one from the way in which I would if nobody had forced me to face the absolute world. That, I fear, is as far as I get towards a solution. I believe there are these two worlds living together and that Christianity does present unfulfillable absolutes to those who listen to it.

McCULLOCH

I'm absolutely in agreement with you; I can't argue with you, because it is true. I think Jesus, when he used those words, did it deliberately. I am sure he knew that we would always have this dilemma. That we would have to match the

world that is struggling to be born with the world that is—
it belongs really to the past, and the tyranny of the past has
somehow to be overcome by what is within ourselves. Is
that not true?

POWELL

You are offering me, as it were, an evolution from this
world, and its contradictions and contrasts with the injunctions of Christianity, into another. I confess I find that
difficult too. Let me take, for example, the very famous
saying about the tribute money: 'Is it lawful to give tribute
unto Caesar?' (Matt 22.17). Very well, here are two political
questions. There is a tax question, you might say. What
ought to be the maximum rate of direct taxation on personal
income? Is it to be as high as 19s. 3d. in the pound or 20s. 6d.
in the pound? That's one implicit question. The other
implicit question is, what ought our position as a subject
nation to be? Ought we to rebel against the imposition of
taxation by a foreign power? I wonder if we don't often
misunderstand the answer which was given. The answer that
was given, 'render under Caesar the things that are Caesar's,'
didn't answer the questions. Christ didn't say, as I understand it: Yes, if that's duly authorized by the latest Finance
Act, then of course 8s. 3d. standard rate it must be. On the
contrary, I take his answer to be: Your entire question is
irrelevant to anything that I have to tell you, and there is
no deduction that you can draw in favour of 8s. 3d. in the
pound or 15s. in the pound, in favour of accepting the
Roman rule or revolting against the Romans. I know everyone has their own interpretation; but to me it seems as
absolute as that.

McCULLOCH

You cannot be wrong in your interpretations because it is
very deliberately shown to us, each in our situation, to
interpret that as we are guided to know what the answer is.
So it would seem to me that he was saying: All right, you
are in a political situation, you must decide for yourself. It
is quite clear that God requires absolutes, as you have so

rightly said. You must learn to find out what is inside your-self to approximate to that absolute. Is that correct?

POWELL

I find that your reference to 'what is inside yourself' is becoming helpful to me. I do at any rate hope that the inside of a person who is constantly confronted with these absolutes and reminded of their existence will be—perhaps this is just a hope—somehow different from the inside of a person who isn't. Yet I don't see how you can predict, given that different inside, what sort of answer he will return on the issues which torment us: taxation, the share of the government and the politician in the direction of the economy and the life of society. That must be something, I would have thought, forever riddling.

Let me explain by means of an analogy, which I mention *only* as an analogy. Say there was a man who was deeply sensitive to music, who felt a great deal of what Beethoven was feeling and saying in the Symphonies. We would all say, this is a different sort of man, there is something different about him, from someone who is tone-deaf and doesn't care if there is music in the world or not. We would say the same about poetry. If we were asked which is the better man, and which man's judgement we would rather respect in the great decisions of personal or of national life, rightly or wrongly we would probably plump for the man who was the more aware. I picture it to myself, under that analogy, that men who are constantly made aware of that other world, that other world of the absolutes and the inscrutables, must surely be somehow, though indefinably, different, and that we would all say they must be somehow better for taking the crucial decisions of national life. I feel I daren't go beyond that; I've ventured perhaps too much.

MCCULLOCH

It so happens that Jesus didn't just say these various things individually; he said them in a general pattern. He said: 'Seek ye first the Kingdom of God' (Matt. 6.33), which presumably presupposes a general pattern of absolute standards that we can all seek. I would have thought that all your questions could have been related in that context to something we could all find and agree upon. I suppose there is a standard of equality before God, of freedom in action, that we could agree upon in that context. Would you think so?

POWELL

Equality before God seems to me to be implicit in Christianity, though not only in Christianity. But where do we go from there? The very qualification or addition, 'before God', switches off all other sorts of equality or inequality. When we say that rich and poor are equal before God we may have stated a truth, but we have not stated anything which will help us, on questions about legislation, to decide between the policy of redistributing income so as to reduce inequality or the policy of maintaining an economy in which inequalities increase though the standard at the bottom may rise, or a policy of using the power of the State to equalize the economic demands which all the members of the State can exercise. These are three forms of society; and you might say that the modern world is embattled, fighting, arguing about these alternatives. Equality before God doesn't help us to select one or the other of them.

McCULLOCH

I'm entirely with you. I've been with you all the way so far. I want to raise a question, however. For my part I have found no difficulty in knowing what it means to say, 'equal before God'; but that may be my sort of stupidity or naiveness. 'Before God' means simply that, in the presence of the universal mystery of life and all that is behind it, I cannot see that any one individual is intrinsically any more important than another, whatever the press may say. I think you are a much more distinguished person than I am, but I suspect God is looking at us quite dispassionately and judging for himself. This I think is true of the whole world. Therefore I would suggest that, although we come into the world with gross inequalities, what we are aiming at in our life and in our politics is to rub out those inequalities or redress the balance so that the strong, or whatever the word should be—the New Testament uses the word strong— carry the weak. Is that right?

POWELL

It may be right, but I cannot see that it is a deduction which can be drawn from 'equality before God'. I may confront a person far poorer than myself or far richer than myself, less or more powerful in the political or social scale, I may confront a man who is my enemy, a national enemy whom I am attempting to destroy, I may confront all these with the conviction that they and I are equally in need of salva- tion, that we are equally powerless to help ourselves, that we are equal in the sight of God in the sense in which you define it; yet I shall not be helped one jot thereby to deduce either an economic policy or a policy for altering or leaving intact the social structure of the nation or a foreign policy which may sacrifice what is regarded as the security or integrity of what people feel is a nation. There lies a gulf, it seems to me, between the one assertion and the other, unless that gulf is bridged, as I tried to suggest, by the fact that men who are penetrated with the conviction of their own ultimate worthlessness, unless that worth comes to them from elsewhere, must surely somehow—but how to predict or define how?—behave differently from the way in which they would behave if they were convinced that there was no other world, no other aspect.

McCULLOCH

Don't let's give our case away. We do agree, both of us, that there is a universe that is a moral universe and makes imperatives upon us. We do agree there, don't we?

POWELL

I'll take another of those imperatives again to illustrate my difficulty. Here is, I suppose, the most absolute imperative, with which we are constantly confronted in the terms of the 'second commandment', to 'love thy neighbour as thy- self' (p. 46). This I take to mean what it says. I do not take it to mean, 'you ought to be a little more kindly than you

are'; or, 'you ought to be a little more charitable than you
are', or, 'you ought to increase your subscriptions by—well
—50 per cent above their present level'. I take it to mean
exactly what it says—which is something impossible,
humanly impossible, for a being with all the instincts of
self-preservation, and all their effects, which are part of
human nature.

McCulloch

Before we go any further, I think this was one of the subtlest
things that was ever said, because it raises the question
whether I really do love *myself*. This is the problem the
Church has never quite solved and has struggled all
through its centuries to solve—whether in fact I love myself.
It presupposes, and rather cleverly, that I do love myself;
but I'm not sure I do, because most of us who love ourselves seem to do ourselves most harm. What we are saying
is, 'are you sure you love yourself? Then, if you *are* sure,
treat your neighbour like that'.

Powell

At least you find that the individuality of any living human
being, the sense of preservation of the individual, struggles
against any such identification and sharing of identity with
the other man and with other men. Therein seems to me to
lie another of those absolutes and impossibles. However,
what I wanted was to use this particular absolute command
—if you'll forgive me still using the word 'absolute', I don't
think you've disagreed with my use of it?

McCulloch
No.

Powell

—to show the difficulty and indeed impracticability of
drawing deductions for political action. If we are to draw
deductions from this command, then we would say that
politically and nationally we ought to treat all human
beings alike. Now, no nation on the face of the earth does
this. No nation on the face of the earth, for example, automatically admits within its frontiers or into its community

those who originate in other communities, as it would admit or readmit its own people. All communities, whatever the particular rules in which they enshrine their methods of action, do in fact draw a basic distinction between their own people and other people. Now, this must be a contradiction of the command to love thy neighbour as thyself. If that applies, for example, to a Pakistani presenting himself at London Airport, it must apply to a Frenchman presenting himself at London Airport. If one then appeals to an Act of Parliament, and says: 'Ah yes, but I've been reading the various Acts of Parliament, or I've been looking up the common law, and I discover that they say one thing about a Pakistani and another about a Frenchman', then one has completely blocked off all claim to make social and political deductions from the absolute command to treat all men alike.

McCULLOCH
Yes; this is, I think, a sound and incontrovertible argument. In all your arguments—and I think this is one of the most admirable things, if I may say so—I'm delighted to find a politician who tries to relate the absolute to the relative. It is obvious that all politicians are faced with the mistakes of their predecessors, and also perhaps with their achievements, if there were any—although most politicians seem to think that anyone who went before was entirely mistaken. Every politician enters into a situation where the mistakes have been made, for lack of judgement, or careful forethought, and so on. 'Statesmen are rare, politicians are many'—this I agree. Now the question is: 'What are you to honour in this situation, trying to keep your absolutes clear, knowing that hospitality is above all things the essence of man, that you *must* show kindness and hospitality to those who need it from you?' The question is, 'how you can do this in a situation which has, for instance, not provided enough beds for the guests'. This surely is where you are, isn't it?

POWELL
While protesting, in a footnote, against the word 'statesman'

being used as superior to 'politician'—I regard 'politician' as the more honourable term, being the name of a caste and a calling, whereas 'statesman' is a rather smarmy word which we put around—

MCCULLOCH
I beg your pardon for using a smarmy word.

POWELL
—I think, Rector, that you rather begged the question by introducing the notion of the mistakes of our predecessors, the mistakes of previous politicians and previous governments. I wasn't on that point. It's easy, if you are satisfied that a mistake has been made, to argue for correcting it or for altering the policy. That isn't the difficulty. The difficulty is with policies—for example, of the nation recognizing its own and those who are not its own—which, whether current or not, whether mistaken or not, whether convenient or not, inevitably do draw distinctions between the treatment of one human being and another human being, distinctions which cannot be derived from, or (I would have thought) in any way justified by, one of the central and absolute commandments of Christianity. Now, I do believe that we in this country have made mistakes in the sphere of politics, in our law which governs the identification of our own people, something which every nation carries out in its own way; and I believe that those mistakes, which have been mistakes of omission—we won't go into them in detail—have brought actual suffering already and threaten more suffering and confusion in the future. However, mistakes are one thing, and the principle is another; and the very principle implicit in nationhood, in statehood, seems to me to be an affront to the injunction to treat all men alike through treating all men 'as oneself'. You say: 'But there is a duty of hospitality; there is a duty of kindness; if a man is within your power, human beings recognize, and upon the whole approve of, those who behave kindly rather than brutally'. So indeed they do; but what has that to do with loving one's neighbour as oneself? The moral duty to be kind rather than unkind, to be civilized rather than brutal, is not specifically Christian,

and is not derivable from the Christian command to love one's neighbour as oneself.

MCCULLOCH

That's right in spirit, and I admire it, but I just want to ask one or two things that you may condemn as irrelevant. May I ask you a personal question? Do you welcome streams of other traditions, races and so on into this particular amalgam of the United Kingdom?

POWELL

I must answer you quantitatively. If they are relatively small, yes; if they are relatively great, no—the same answer as is given by every other nation on the face of the earth in the same circumstances. Then you say to me: 'What do you mean by small, and what do you mean by great?' I cannot produce for you a standard (that's the word you used much earlier in this dialogue) from which you can read off the right percentage; otherwise my job as a politician wouldn't need doing at all. If we could have automatic rules which could automatically be applied, it would be plain sailing. I have to exercise judgement, and I have to secure general support for the implementation of that judgement in terms of law and for its enforcement with the power of the state. In doing so, I am doing, as I have to do, my job; but I cannot justify my outlook, my letter of the law, or even my nationhood from these searching, absolute assertions and commands of Christianity. I have to take refuge in other directions. I have to say: 'Presumably God not only created me as I am individually—insofar as I am an individual; for that is an abstraction—but as belonging to a family or society or nation, which is as much reality as anything about me, or about the world or about any of the rest of the creation.' I start therefore from the presumption that all this is inherently natural in human terms. There again, I find myself looking across this gulf, which one looks across down there (*pointing to the altar*), between one world and another; and when you reach out your hand to bridge that gulf, you receive something which can mean nothing or everything.

McCULLOCH

I'll try and respect that answer. You don't give the answer I wanted, which would clear a lot of the confusion out of what you've been saying in public for a long time. Still, when I asked you: 'Do you welcome the enrichment of guests and fellow-citizens from all over the world or other traditions?' you said yes. I don't want to dispute numbers. That's a political matter, isn't it? I don't want to dispute any of those things, because they must be settled by those who are in charge of such affairs. All I wanted to know was—and I've got the answer—that you did welcome the enrichment of all manner of folk, if we have room for them, and if we can see our way to making a happy family of people of all kinds in this island. Is that correct?

POWELL

You have put quite a number of words into my mouth. You inserted the word 'enrichment'. Now I would not presume as a politican, considering the entry into this country for settlement of small numbers of persons, to make cultural judgements such as are implied in the word 'enrichment'. I don't believe that politicians or the state have the right to make and impose that sort of qualitative judgement. I would much rather put it negatively, which may be disappointing to you, and say that I cannot see this as an evil which must be prevented, so self-evidently harmful that I want to use the power of the state to say no, rather than to say yes. (Of course, I'm presuming that the state *has* armed itself with the power to say no or yes, as it has done at last in this country and as all other countries have always done.) The second imputation which you put into my mouth, and which I wouldn't wish to accept, is that you seem to put far greater emphasis than I do on objective factors, of space, employment, housing, and so on. I don't believe that that is the heart of the matter. After all we've grown from a nation of fifteen million to thirty million, from thirty million to fifty million, without taking any harm from it—at least *I* don't think so—and I see no reason why we shouldn't grow from a nation of fifty million to seventy million ...

MCCULLOCH
But you aren't answering ...

POWELL
But you see what I said—grow from a *nation* of fifty million to a *nation* of seventy million. So I've introduced the political, non-Christian concept of the nation; and politics if not wholly, at any rate very largely, is about nations. Therefore my judgement would be exercised in the light of what I thought was the nation and what involved the future of the nation.

MCCULLOCH
That's the real statement, which I nevertheless think has brought you and me close together in sentiment. I expected to meet a highly intelligent man—and I certainly did that— but I was dubious about whether I would meet a kind man. I *have* met a kind man, and I'm very grateful. I think, despite the utterances that are reported in the Press, we are greatly privileged to have met a very remarkable person and one I would like to talk to for a very long time indeed.

11

CHRISTIANITY AND IMMIGRATION

I

Dialogue with Douglas Brown[1]

BROWN

Mr Powell, I don't want to trick you or provoke you in any
way. All I want to do is to find out more about your thinking and your beliefs, bearing in mind your two speeches on
immigration[2] and the fact that you're a practising Christian
—in fact, you are a member of the Church of England, I
believe, a High Church Anglican, and you attend church
regularly. Yet, funnily, the strongest criticism of your Eastbourne speech has come from leaders of your own Church.
Now has this prompted you to have second thoughts?

POWELL

No. Could I say first to you, in order to put into context
what is called the first of my two speeches on immigration,
that I have been writing and speaking on this subject for
several years, and that, although these last two speeches—at
Birmingham and at Eastbourne—attracted far more attention than the others, it would be wrong to think that this is
a subject which I have suddenly picked up and blown up
into a public issue, or an issue that I specially wish to speak
on? Now you ask me about the fact that so many leaders,
not only of the Anglican Church but of other churches, have
condemned in various ways and on various grounds what
I've said. I don't account for that on religious grounds, any

[1] 1 December 1968, BBC Radio 4.
[2] Birmingham, 20 April, and Eastbourne, 16 November 1968.

more than I account on religious grounds for the fact that many journalists who perhaps have no religious belief have similarly attacked me. I think that the reaction of the writers and speakers, including church writers and speakers, has been one more evidence of the staggering and dangerous gap between what is known by personal experience to a few millions of people, who live in the areas affected, and is somehow sensed by the great majority of the population, and what it seems possible to bring home to the small minority—of course it's bound to be a small minority—who speak and write. I regard the bishops as typical of that small minority, who are on the other side of this comprehension gap.

BROWN
Let us take these criticisms one by one for a moment. The Archbishop of Canterbury has described your remarks as, 'the counsel of despair'. What do you think about that?

POWELL
I would indeed despair if I thought it inevitable that the immigrant and immigrant-descended population of this country would continue to grow till it was (shall we say?) approximately five million by the end of the century. That prospect gives the urgency in my mind to the taking now of measures which I believe to be practicable—it's a different issue whether they are or not, but I believe them to be practicable—which could avoid that happening.

BROWN
And do you believe these measures are motivated by Christian thinking?

POWELL
Measures are a means to an end. So we must look at the end. The end is to avoid a situation arising in this country which I believe would be catastrophic and, as I have said over and over again, just as dangerous and damaging to the immigrants and their descendants as to the indigenous population. None of the measures which I and my Party have proposed in order to deal with this seems to me to be

open to objection on moral grounds. Let's look at some of them. Voluntary repatriation. Now we can argue—I am willing to argue—about the potential scope of this measure. But how can it be immoral or objectionable to assist a person who wishes to return to his own country, or indeed to go to another country—to re-emigrate—to do so? Control of the inflow. Well, we are all, I think, now agreed that the inflow of new immigrants should be controlled and brought to very small proportions. So, if there is a moral issue here, it's a moral issue in which everybody is on the same side. Finally, the question of the dependants: the right of a person already in this country to have his dependants, as defined, join him. (Of course, you do appreciate that this right doesn't apply to all dependants? For instance, it isn't a right in respect of elderly parents. That's only a concession. The right only applies to wives and children up to a certain age.) Now, I agree here that you are faced with an alternative. You are faced, if you like, with a choice of evils; for the dependants are the source of the future growth of population, being preponderantly women and children. Therefore, one has to ask which is the greater danger, which course will do more harm, or offer more risk to the people concerned: to reduce now the basis for a future growth of the immigrant or immigrant-descended population, or to say to a person who is already here: 'You came here in certain circumstances; those circumstances have now changed. We regret this, but we are taking a course which we believe is the lesser evil.'

BROWN
That kind of regret, surely, isn't the question, is it? We encouraged these people here in the first place.

POWELL
No, we didn't encourage them. That's not correct, if by 'we' you mean the nation. This thing happened because until 1962 the law of this country could not distinguish between a British subject born in, or (if you like) belonging to, this country, and the hundreds of millions living in the former British Empire. They came because nobody could, as it were,

see them coming. As an immigrant before 1962 entered this country he was indistinguishable in the law of this country from you or me coming back from a weekend in Paris.

BROWN
Indistinguishable save for his colour.

POWELL
No, no. He was indistinguishable in law. At the point of entry he had exactly the same right to enter. Then in 1962, for the first time, this country did what every other country has always done—defined the people who belong to itself—and thus for the first time enabled itself to control the inflow of Commonwealth citizens who do not—I still must use this broad expression—'belong' to the United Kingdom. So, when you say we encouraged these people to come, what would be correct is to say that 'we'—whether that means the nation, the government, or Parliament—left the law unamended while they were coming. That's very different.

BROWN
Mr Powell, how do you belong to the United Kingdom? How do you establish yourself, for instance, as an Englishman?

POWELL
If I may say so, that—I'm not being impertinent—is one of those silly questions, which are difficult when one asks for a definition but to which everybody knows the answer. Of course, we do—we always have done—naturalize in this country—first of all, by a specific act of naturalization, a legal act, and secondly, by the process of time, by the succession of the generations—people who are initially alien, so that they become amalgamated into the population of this country. Of course, too, the population of this country contains infinite varieties, strands and strains. Yet that it is a homogenous population, and that in Britain a German or a Russian or a Chinese or a Philippino is an alien and not an Englishman, is not open to doubt. And the same would be said by every other nation under the sun.

BROWN
But wouldn't you say that a first generation West Indian
or first generation Asian is just as much an Englishman as
I'm an Englishman or you're an Englishman, or perhaps a
Welshman?

POWELL
Clearly not.

BROWN
If not the first generation, then the children of the first
generation?

POWELL
How can this be so? Let's take another example, where
colour doesn't enter into it, and then move across to the
case before us, where colour *is* one of the elements, though
not the *only* element, because, of course, a West Indian is
not a European whose skin is darker, but belongs to a different race, and has other different characteristics. However,
let's take an instance first where race or colour is not
involved. Let us suppose the settlement in this country not
just of one family but of hundreds of thousands of Germans.
Let us suppose that hundreds of thousands of Germans,
because our law didn't distinguish between Hanoverians and
British—that could have happened!—had settled in this
country in four or five areas having children and bringing
them up speaking German in a German community. Now,
would one say that those children, because they have been
born in England, are Englishmen and not Germans? Of
course we know many cases where a German family
settling here and the children have ceased over the years to
regard themselves as preponderantly German, and become
more and more assimilated in outlook and in background
to the rest of the people of the country. Yet even for them
it is a slow process; and you know how, in time of war,
when people are being commissioned for certain functions,
we look not only to their birth but to their ancestry. Having
established this in a case where colour doesn't enter at all,
look at the present situation, with a population coming from
cultures and from areas infinitely more remote in almost

every way you can imagine from those of the United Kingdom, than the German case which I imagined. Surely it's absurd to say, except in a legal sense, that a child of a West Indian family living here in a West Indian community, or a child of a Punjabi family living here in a Punjabi community, is just as much an English child as your children or mine. You know, when we defy reality by making a statement like that, I don't think we are being generous, or idealistic. I think we are being dangerous, because to defy reality—certainly for a politician—is the most dangerous thing we can do.

BROWN

Am I being unrealistic when I think that you are arguing racial purity?

POWELL

No, I'm not talking about race at all. I am talking about those differences, some of which are related to race, between the members of different nations which make the assimilation of the members of one nation into another nation more difficult or less difficult. I can perfectly well see that it might be easier for an individual Indian family than for a German family to be assimilated into an English background and become after one, two or three generations indistinguishably English. Yet we cannot deny the fact that external marks of difference are very important, because they enable men to mark the existence of those other characteristics, which are not visible but which do differentiate one nation from another and one man or family alien in another environment.

BROWN

But surely this is the question: Should we as Christians be conscious of these differences?

POWELL

Now we've come to the issues. I do not doubt that in Christ all men are equal. We say they are 'equal in the sight of God'. Note, by the way, that this doesn't apply only to Commonwealth citizens. If any deduction is to be drawn for immigration policy from the proposition that all men are equal in Christ, then it must apply to Frenchmen, to Germans, to Russians, to Chinese, to Philippinos. I can see the argument of the man who says: 'There should be no frontiers; there should be no nations; there should be no customs barriers, no passports, because all men are equal in Christ'. I can begin to follow that argument. But I cannot follow the argument of the man who says on religious grounds: 'We ought to admit people who are defined by our domestic law' (of which the law of Christ knows nothing) 'in one way, but not those whom it defines in another.'

BROWN
If we believe that Christ is all in all and that we should be motivated in all we do by Christian belief, then surely there is no argument: all men are equal.

POWELL
Yes, but if then you deduce from this that all men have an equal right to enter the United Kingdom whatever be their origin, then you must not apply that only to people who happen to come from territories formerly parts of the British Empire. The law of Christ knows nothing of that; it knows nothing of the British Empire; it knows nothing of nations and nationalities at all. You must keep open house for all the nations—for the Europeans, for the Chinese, for the Americans, for the South Americans.

BROWN
Surely if you are a true Christian, you do just that?

POWELL
In that case there is no nation upon the face of the earth, and there is no political party in this country, which follows what you say is true Christianity. If I may say so, I think you have brought our conversation to the verge of a great divide: the divide between the world of Christ and Christianity and this world. The world of Christ and Christianity is a world, humanly speaking, of impossibilities. It is a world in which bread is flesh, and wine is blood. It is a world in which you are commanded to do the impos-

sible—not just to love your neighbour, (that's not what you are commanded to do) but to love your neighbour 'as yourself', which is for man—humanly speaking—impossible. The commands of Christianity are in this sense supernatural, that they are by definition unfulfillable to men in this world, as Christ contrasted it with the Kingdom of heaven. I don't see how you can deduce an immigration policy from these commands and truths of Christianity. I do not see how you can conduct in accordance with them the affairs of nations, which require that you distinguish between those who are your own people and those who are other people— distinguish economically, distinguish politically, and in the end—quoting the 37th Article—'as Christian men wear weapons, and serve in the wars.' You cannot deduce the right or wrong in such behaviour.

BROWN
Surely Christianity is a religion of gentleness and compassion? Surely above all else we must show to these people this compassion, even if it means for many of us living uncomfortably for a number of years, even if we do have to have large alien quarters, large alien groupings, in our midst? Otherwise what does Christianity mean?

POWELL
Well, many others besides Christians regard compassion as a proper quality of a man, and I would not say that to be compassionate, or to recognize the duty to be compassionate, is uniquely or specifically Christian. But leaving that on one side, if I thought that the future held an immigrant and immigrant-descended population in this country of approximately the present size, I'd be a very happy man indeed. But if I am right in thinking that without measures that are not yet understood, let alone in course of being prepared and taken, the growth in that population will be such than an intolerable tension will be set up in this country, a tension as dangerous to the immigrant as to the rest of the nation, then is it not compassionate for me as a politician to point to this and say: 'Look, here is a danger, which you can avoid but to which you are inexorably moving'? I would

claim that the man who, even in the face of misunderstanding and abuse and vilification, still goes on drawing the attention of his fellow men to what he believes to be a danger they can avoid, can hardly be regarded as an uncompassionate man. If I wanted strife, if I were a lover of strife, if I wanted to see racial strife and welcomed it, then I would sit back; but I don't feel I can.

BROWN
Obviously you don't believe in a multi-racial society then?

POWELL
We must define a word like that. In all societies there can be, and with advantage, small minorities—how small, must depend upon the nature of the minority and the circumstances—who are differentiated from the rest, not only by language and background, but also by race. If that is what you mean by a multi-racial society, then every society is a multi-racial society, and it is likely that the society of the United Kingdom, with its history and its trading and maritime position in the world, will have probably a larger variety of such minorities than most. But if by a multi-racial society you mean a society which is deliberately and indeed artificially compounded by bringing together masses of people from different backgrounds, different cultures, and implanting them in a nation with a long and continuous history, a nation probably as homogeneous as any there is in the world in its feeling—I'm not talking about physiology but about sentiment—then I believe that the idea is a mischievous and a dangerous one.

BROWN
But couldn't you form a new and exciting society? You don't know, do you? I mean, in Trinidad this has happened. There you have a truly multi-racial society, and Trinidad—I happen to know from personal experience—is a very happy island.

POWELL
Well, you know Trinidad and I don't; but I do know countries in the East, in which different races live together.

But they live together without in any way being members
of the same society. The same national frontier has been
drawn round them—in Singapore there are the Chinese,
there are the Malays, and there are the Indians—but it is
not one society, and I do not believe that any of those
elements believes that it can be, or wishes that it should be.
Just now you said: 'Can we not construct or make or create
a society?' My answer to that is, no. I don't believe that
you do create societies. I believe that this social engineering,
in which a group of people—in this case without consulting
or being understood, let alone supported, by the mass of
their fellow countrymen—say to themselves: 'Let's change
this society; let us implant in it something which is profoundly different and alien; then let us see how it goes', is
criminal levity.

BROWN
Let's turn to something that is really more important:
whatever happens, we're going to have a sizeable coloured
minority staying on here, are we not? From reading I should
think probably it could be something like a million plus.
What do you think our relationship should be with these
people?

POWELL
I'm sorry: I differ entirely. You said: 'Let's turn to something more important'; but you have now made an assumption which, as I said before, would make me the happiest
man in England, if I could share it with you. Of course, if
the present immigrant and immigrant-descended population,
which is about a million and a quarter, were the maximum,
then indeed, as I said in my speech, 'the slow mercy of the
years' would in time obliterate the frictions, the fears, the
anxieties, which have accompanied the events of the last
fifteen years. But so improbable, so unbelievable does that
figure appear to me to be, so clear is it to me that that
is not the situation which we are facing, that, when people
ask me: 'Why aren't you interested in integration or im-
proved relations with this million or a million and a quarter?'
my answer is: 'That is not the problem'. In the areas, and

I represent one of them, where the native population has been most affected by this sudden influx, the tolerance which is shown, and the acceptance of even the present inflow, is something which is an everlasting tribute to the British people. The problem isn't there. The problem lies in the threat of the future. So, forgive me, the problem of race relations in this country—how I hate that expression 'race relations'!—the problem (I would rather say) of the consequences of Commonwealth immigration in this country, is not how this present million and a quarter get on with this present fifty million, but how we can prevent that million and a quarter attaining a size which, linked with their concentration, will be intolerable and unmanageable.

BROWN

What do you mean by an intolerable and unmanageable. You just argued, and argued very pertinently, that the British people are extremely tolerant. Don't you think they could tolerate five million?

POWELL

No. Do you say that those who have seen themselves excluded from a tenth or an eighth or a sixth of their native town, who have seen that part of their native town converted for practical purposes into a part of the Punjab or of the West Indies, will find it equally acceptable, that a quarter, or half, or three-quarters, or the whole, should become a part of the West Indies or of the Punjab? This is the fallacy of arguing that the effect of an inch is the same as the effect of a yard.

BROWN

Mr Powell, one criticism, quite a strong one, that's been made of you, is that you are playing on the fears and prejudices of ignorant and unthinking people, that you're crawling after the biggest vote, as someone put it, that you're gambling on the darker side of human nature to achieve your own political advantages. What do you say to that?

POWELL

My answer is a very simple one. The people who are facing

this themselves know it already. There is no question of my telling the people of Wolverhampton, of Bradford, of Birmingham what they know and see. What I have to do is to bring home the facts which are known in Wolverhampton, in Bradford and in Birmingham, to those who live in palaces and who vote in Parliament, so that they shall realize what the future holds. In order to do that, it is not the people in Wolverhampton I have to frighten or stir up, but the archbishops.

BROWN
Is it true that you don't like coloured people, Mr Powell?

POWELL
I have very little background knowledge of the West Indies and West Indians, but I have considerable background knowledge of the peoples of India and Pakistan. I spent three of some of the best years of my life avidly trying to learn as much as I could about the culture of a part of India. As I have often said, I fell in love with India when I went there. I have no sense of superiority either to an Indian or to a West Indian. Of course, I'm aware of a sense of difference; but that sense of difference is a respect for him, just as it is respect for a Continental European not to think of him as only another sort of Englishman, born the other side of the Channel. All men are entitled to respect in their own right, in their own national background, in their own cultural background. It is a contempt for men to treat them as pawns or counters that can be arranged together in different patterns according to the will of the social engineer.

BROWN
Mr Powell, finally, Christians are always thought of as optimists. Are you optimistic about the future of our society, coloured and white?

POWELL
A man who is warning his fellow countrymen against a danger and asking them to take steps now to avoid it, dare not be optimistic. I don't think it was the business of those who were warning Britain in the 1930s about the danger of

the rearming of Nazi Germany, to be optimistic. I remember that at that time I myself was not optimistic. It's not the business of a captain, trying to save his ship from being driven on to rocks, to be optimistic; it's his business to exert seamanship. It's our business to exert statesmanship.

II
Dialogue with Trevor Huddleston

HUDDLESTON

When I wrote the letter to you, Mr Powell, on the subject of immigration,[1] and when I quoted and talked about evil, I made it clear, I hope, that I wasn't at that stage in any kind of way questioning the sincerity of your motives. What I meant when I said the speech was evil, was this. Having lived and worked in a society in South Africa where racism has become entrenched in a constitutional form, I have seen the dignity of man destroyed by racism. I believe that what you said in your speech intentionally or otherwise was bound to create conditions in this country which would increase tension, racial tension, which would therefore undermine seriously the real dignity of man, and in that sense I believed, and still believe, that it was evil. That was why I particularly wished to be able to give my reasons for thinking this.

POWELL

Of course 'evil' coming from a Bishop—and I'm extremely grateful to you for what you wrote to me, and for what you said just now—tends to have a specifically religious connotation. I'm sure that many politicians in arguing would

[1] On the day after I spoke on immigration at Wolverhampton on 9 June 1969, the Bishop of Stepney publicly referred to the speech as 'evil'. A correspondence ensued between us which led to this discussion.

designate others' proposals or policies as evil; but it is clearly not in that sense that we are talking about evil here. We are, I think, talking about that evil which a Christian, because he is a Christian, has a duty to avoid. Now it seems to me, Bishop—and perhaps you provided a clue in the reference to your South African experience—that you are forming views on political consequences, on social consequences, which indeed anyone might form and anyone might challenge. But that the issue of what would be the effect of what I said, and of the way in which I said it, cannot be a specifically religious issue, and once one has established the intentions with which I acted, the motives with which I acted (which I am quite happy to try and explain further), then from that point onwards moral judgement is suspended and we simply become two citizens comparing prognostications and judgements outside the religious sphere.

HUDDLESTON
I can never agree with that diagnosis of religion. To me religion is not compartmentalized; to me social and political issues are essentially religious issues; and when I talk of evil, I don't know whether I am talking of it in a religious sense or a political sense or a social sense. I am talking of evil, and you quite often use the word evil in your speeches, as a matter of fact. You've used it, if I remember rightly, about the immigration problem. You said that statesmen, or politicians, have got to look ahead, and prevent preventable evils; and I wouldn't admit for a single moment that you can say something is politically evil, but religiously not evil.

POWELL
Certainly a thing can be politically evil if it has damaging consequences in the context in which one is speaking, which might be economic, might be national, or might even be military. My difficulty is that I simply do not see how one can derive a judgement, one way or the other, from what I can best understand, with my limitations, of Christianity. Let me put the question in a sharp form in the

context of this particular issue. I can see that it could be argued that because in the sight of God all men are equal, therefore no difference should be made between one man and another who presents himself at the frontier of the country. But once one accepts that we live in a world of nations, and that we do distinguish between those who belong and don't belong to this or that nation, then it seems to me that any deduction which could be drawn from that basic assertion of Christianity is not available. Do you see my difficulty?

HUDDLESTON

I see your difficulty, but I can't really understand why somebody as intelligent as you has that particular difficulty. It seems to me that the Christian faith is based on one fundamental fact. This is the fact that God became man. He did not become an Englishman, he did not become a Palestinian, he did not become an Irishman. I think he would have found it an impossible situation if he had. He became man, and therefore man as man has an inherent dignity. Now if this dignity is in any kind of way destroyed or damaged, this is a matter where the Christian Church, in my view, has to speak, and I as a Bishop of a Christian Church have to speak. If the people in the part of the diocese of London of which I have charge—and there are a very large number of coloured people there—are affected for the worse by something which is said in a politician's speech, and if, as I believe, the effect of this speech is to create insecurity, to create a feeling of tension, then I am bound to speak out and say so, because for me this is an offence against God; it's not just a political offence or a social or economic lack of understanding; it's an offence against God.

POWELL

You say that if, as you believe, the effect of such propositions is to increase tensions, then you should speak out against it. Indeed I, too, and not as a Bishop, would speak out against anything which I thought was likely to increase tensions. Mistakenly or otherwise, I think I am doing just that; and here I come back to my difficulty. Here are the two of us, not unacquainted with the circumstances which we are talking about, who form different judgements. You as a qualified observer, quite apart from your ecclesiastical character, I as a politician and a Member of Parliament, form different judgements to the best of our ability as to where the dangers in the future lie, and how they are more likely to be banished or diminished. Now, we can argue about this. I can try to convince you of the greater probability of my view, and you vice-versa. But it seems to me that we are purely at a level of opinion, and that our duty towards God and man is only infringed in so far as knowingly and through turpitude I take a course of action which to me is likely nett, overall, to produce more damage to human beings.

HUDDLESTON

Yes, well, you have used the word danger. What is exactly the danger that you see in the presence of the coloured community in this country? I would like to know exactly what is the danger? Is it, as you said on other occasions, the question of numbers only? Why do you feel this to be a danger, when, as you know, for the last six years more people have left this country than entered it?

POWELL

I'm sorry, I thought when you asked 'is it a question of numbers?', you meant the number of immigrants. I don't regard this at all as a question of total numbers of inhabitants of the United Kingdom.

HUDDLESTON

No, this is what I am getting at: why do you feel the presence of a coloured minority group is a danger? This is what I want you to answer.

POWELL

Certainly, and I would have thought that a glance at the world would show how easily tensions leading to violence arise where there is a majority and a minority (who, of course, locally can be inversely the majority and the minority) with sharp differences, recognizable differences, and mutual fears. Now, when the numbers of the minority —no one can be absolute on numbers, but you would not expect that—are small, then this danger hardly exists. It is as the numbers of the minority (which in some areas is the majority) rise, that the danger grows. Consequently the whole of this issue to me, from the beginning, is one of number. I don't mean that number is the only factor, but that it is the key factor.

Going back to what I said earlier, it seems to me that I can't derive from any tenets of Christianity any conclusion as to the tolerable number in a given case, which a politician, in pursuance of his duty should countenance. If we are to deduce from the tenets of Christianity that all men are to be treated alike, then the argument would carry us very much further. We shall throw open all frontiers, we shall say that all men are literally brothers, and that nations have been abolished. This I can see. But as long as we retain frontiers, and national identification, and as long as people do in fact feel as national communities (a thing easier to say than define), this is something of which I feel I am duty bound to take account; and I can't feel that taking account of it is in conflict with anything that I understand of Christian duty. I can't see any deduction that I have to make as to the Commonwealth Immigrants Acts, or the British Nationality Act, from the principles of Christianity.

HUDDLESTON
Well, you said you take a glance at the world, and you see these tensions building up as a result of a kind of conflict in numbers—a minority group, or minority groups, becoming majority groups, and so forth. Now I have taken a glance at the world and come to the exact opposite conclusion, because I have spent most of my life in South Africa. I know the effect, if I may say so, of your speeches, on millions of Africans in the newly independent countries of Africa. This question of race and colour conflict is not a local conflict. I absolutely understand that as M.P. for Wolverhampton you are thinking of your constituents, you are thinking of a particular situation. You may be thinking

of the country as a whole; but even taking it that the number of coloured immigrants increases to the maximum that you have ever envisaged, it is still a minority group in a country which has got a very long tradition of liberal, democratic principle behind it—a minority group, which on any showing cannot become a majority group in this country.

POWELL
Not everywhere, no.

HUDDLESTON
Not everywhere, no.... And yet in the world as a whole, we have the makings of the third World War along colour lines every time a speech is made in this country by a responsible politician on race lines, as it appears. (I don't want to pre-judge your motives, but certainly to an African nation, newly independent, just thrown off colonialism, it is the way it does appear, and I can speak from absolute first-hand experience.) This is to me the only way we can look at this situation. Here in England, in point of fact, I would say, we have no problem. If we have, then we are a very flabby nation indeed. If we really maintain that we cannot accept the presence of a minority group of, let us say, ten million coloured people in a total in A.D. 2000 of seventy million, then we have not really learnt what the world is about, we haven't learnt what way the world is moving, we are still bogged down in a completely little-Englander, isolationist view of world affairs.

I believe this brings us back to the point of Christianity. If Christianity is a universal faith, Christianity is not a faith which has its main strength in the West, although it has numerically. It is a universal, Catholic faith, and therefore must be concerned with this issue on a world basis. It cannot concern itself with what happens only in Wolverhampton, and similar places, and if it does, then it's failing as a faith. Now I am not unsympathetic. I quite understand from your point of view that you have got to take account of people's views and opinions. I believe you are mistaken. I believe that Britain today, as a matter of fact, has got far more tolerant people in it on this issue of race than you give reason to suppose, from your speeches, and I believe it is the duty of a responsible politician to build on this tolerance, and not to increase the intolerance which is certainly there.

POWELL

Certainly I wouldn't do anything which I thought likely to increase intolerance; but you have produced, I thought, two very important issues. I would like to take the second one, but to me the lesser, first. You said that something said in British conditions and with regard to British conditions can have a quite different and perhaps incalculable effect when it is reported somewhere else, when it is interpreted somewhere else, in the light of conditions which exist in that somewhere else. I quite agree. But then I have a conflict of duty. If I think something requires to be said in the interests of the community to which I belong that is necessary to be said, heard, and if possible acted on, then it seems to me that, even to begin to carry out that duty, I have to choose the lesser evil and accept the consequences of the more indirect and distant reaction (which, indeed, will partly be based upon misapprehension). So here is a typical situation for a politician, as I think for most men: a choice of evils, a choice of courses of action, both of which are fraught with disadvantages. My answer is that I cannot see that it is wrong for me to prefer what I believe to be the advantage of those to whom I am more directly responsible in my capacity of politician and Member of Parliament.

So that's the first dilemma which, if I may say so, you've exposed: I don't think I can—either of us, perhaps—resolve it. But the second goes deeper.

You say that you believe that the dangers which I think I see are largely unreal, that you believe there are far more reserves of tolerance than I dare presume. Here again, I am in a very typical situation for a politician. A politician would wish that human nature, and the human nature of his own people, was perhaps better than he supposed it to be; but unless he acts upon his judgement of what it is—a

judgement which may be mistaken—it seems to me that he
is guilty of a betrayal.

May I take a parallel—it's a fair parallel, perhaps—from
a quite different area altogether? I happen to be opposed to
capital punishment. I've consistently voted against capital
punishment for murder. Now the reason why I've done this
is because I do not believe that it is a deterrent. But, if I had
believed it was a deterrent, and had nevertheless voted against
it, because I thought people ought to learn to be less violent,
less prone to murder, then I would in my view be betraying
my duty as a politician and a representative. I think that
this kind of dilemma runs through human nature: the
dilemma between human nature as it is presented to us in
Christ, and human nature as we know it and as it is the datum
of political action.

HUDDLESTON
I think when you talk about the best interests of this country,
this is the point I am trying to make. I don't think that the
best interests of this country are served, in fact, by treating
this issue of race and colour conflict on a local, purely
national basis. This is a world issue. And therefore you
ought to think (may I dare to say so?), before you speak,
of its effect on the greater part of mankind, which is the
coloured part of mankind. And this is where I take issue
with you. I think in fact you are building up a situation of
tension which is highly dangerous for this country. We have
already lost of course millions of friends, in Africa and
Asia, because of our attitude on the issues which to them
are vital, like Rhodesia. We have already, in fact, lost a
credit which we had at the moment when these countries
became independent, precisely because of this kind of
speech, and I believe that you are not serving the best
interests of your country when you make this kind of speech,
because racism is a burning issue in every part of the world,
of Africa and of Asia. This is something every politician
must know—that is, unless he's very stupid, and you're
certainly not that.

But I would like to come back again to this point that

Great Britain is desperately seeking some form of national goal or purpose. I cannot believe that we are a nation that is so dim and stupid that we cannot see this national purpose in terms of our place in the world community. I believe that this is where our energies have to lie. Internationalism, the unification of the world, is the next stage and is already coming about, whether we like it or not, by mass communication. In this whole picture we have a role to play which we are not playing, or rather which we are playing disastrously, because we are alienating the majority of mankind by our deliberate immoral choices and actions.

The British, you see, have in their history, through the colonial expansion, and in every possible way, quite deliberately moved into other people's countries, have created and sustained regimes, power, over African and Asian people for many years at a time, have called upon those people to fight with them in their wars, to die for them. We have done all this, we have at a certain point in our history taken a deliberate part in the slave trade which has created the West Indies, and yet when three million Africans and Asians come to this country, many of whom come at our express desire to help our economy, we say: 'No, you are "an alien wedge" '.

POWELL

I could wish that the admission of Commonwealth citizens to this country had indeed been a deliberate act—for instance, for economic reasons, as we have imported Italian labour into the brick-fields, and elsewhere. The tragedy was that our law of citizenship in this country did not enable us to do any such thing. It isn't that the door was open or shut; there literally was no door. We are not in a position in which previous acts of government, deliberate acts, by which a certain immigration was authorized and organized, have produced a certain situation which could then be foreseen or ought to have been foreseen. On the contrary, we are seeing the consequences of having lived too long—I accept as a politician that my profession is to blame for it—with a completely unreal law of citizenship in this country. And we now have to consider how far the consequences and implicit dangers, as we respectively see them, of that largely inadvertent act, can be modified or even reversed.

HUDDLESTON
It wasn't inadvertent really, was it, because we deliberately recruited West Indies labour at a time we needed it to do the dirty work.

POWELL
Who is the 'we'?

HUDDLESTON
The British Government.

POWELL
Oh, no! This, as a matter of fact, is not the case.

HUDDLESTON
The transport services of this country are nationalized services, and we recruited West Indians quite deliberately to run the transport services of this country and the hospital services.

POWELL
The Government could not have prevented this recruitment, had it so wished, without a fundamental change in our citizenship law first taking place. It does seem to me very misleading to say that because there was no distinction, in the then state of our law, between the inhabitants of the four continents which were formerly part of the British Empire and the people who belong to the United Kingdom, therefore the inevitable recruitment by private and by publicly owned industry which followed was a deliberate act of state.

HUDDLESTON
Well, I would agree that we need a new definition of citizenship. I don't suppose the definition that I want is the same as yours, but I agree with this wholeheartedly, we certainly do need a new definition of citizenship in this country badly.

But we need a definition of citizenship which carries with it inescapably the full rights of citizenship, and what I still want to know from you, really, is why the presence of a coloured immigrant group is objectionable, when the presence of a non-coloured immigrant group is not objectionable.

POWELL
On the contrary, I have often said that if we saw the prospect of five million Germans in this country at the end of the century, the risks of disruption and violence would probably be greater, and the antagonism which would be aroused would be more severe. The reason why the whole debate in this country on immigration is related to coloured immigration is because there has been no net immigration of white Commonwealth citizens, and there could be no uncontrolled immigration of aliens. This is merely an automatic consequence of the facts of the case. It is not because there is anything different or necessarily more dangerous about the alienness of a community from Asia, than about the alienness of a community from Turkey or from Germany, that we discuss this inevitably in terms of colour. It is because it is that problem.

HUDDLESTON
Yes, well, our history has been a history of immigration as well as a history of emigration; we have had a wave of immigrants far in excess of five million all over the period.

POWELL
When was this?

HUDDLESTON
Well through our history, we have Irish immigrants, Italian immigrants, over the long stretch of history. You were talking about foreseeing things.

POWELL
Possibly so, but is there any real analogy?

HUDDLESTON
There is a very real analogy. Why if this 'alien wedge' that

you spoke of recently in a speech....

POWELL
Actually I was using the words of a Lord of Appeal.[2]

HUDDLESTON
I don't care who he was.

POWELL
Well, they are not this politician's words; they are words of a man who spent his life drafting judgements.

HUDDLESTON
Yes, maybe, but this 'alien wedge', quite demonstrably in your speech, referred to a coloured alien wedge.

POWELL
It couldn't be otherwise, because it's the only 'alien wedge' we are concerned with.

HUDDLESTON
Well, unless you are prepared to concede that the Irish, for instance, are immigrants; we have got a good many of them in this country who have been absorbed perfectly well. We have still a very large Jewish community (thank God) in this country, which have been absorbed perfectly well. Why is there, then, this sudden trauma?

POWELL
I think you've failed to see the essential importance of numbers and time. That factor has been utterly different in these other cases, unless one goes back to the Scandinavian invasions in the tenth century.

HUDDLESTON
But they haven't in relation to the total population of this country. As I have said already, I would be perfectly happy if there might be ten million coloured people in this country at the end of this century, and I would thank God for it, because it would at least bring some fresh blood into a very tired old country.

[2] Viscount Radcliffe G.B.E., in the Carr Saunders Memorial Lecture delivered to the Institute of Race Relations in February 1969.

POWELL

Well then, you see, Bishop, we get back to a comparison of judgements as to the future; and because my judgement differs on the likelihoods and possibilities and dangers, I cannot feel (as I understand that you say I should) that I am acting against my Christian duty in drawing attention to what I think I see.

HUDDLESTON

Well, I'll grant you your principles, but what I will not grant you is your lack of perception, because, when you speak about an 'alien wedge', you are actually speaking about millions of people who are actually in this country, who are a permanent part of this country, who happen to be coloured. By so speaking, you increase their insecurity enormously, and you do very great damage, if I may say so. I don't care what the actual figure is. Whatever proportion of those are going to stay, are affected by what you say about 'alien wedge'; and when you talk about danger, when you talk about evil, in respect of immigrant presences here, they are affected by it. These are people that I have a direct responsibility for, and I know they suffer.

POWELL

And they are people for whom I also in my sphere have a direct responsibility; and I will oppose, since this is a secular issue, my judgement to yours. First, I will say that those who intend to stay fear most the consequences of an increasing rise in the total numbers, because they fear the reaction upon them and their future which would result. That is why I always say that I consider myself to be speaking and acting on behalf of all my constituents. But secondly, it is not true to say of a very considerable element (nobody could say how large, and it will apply more to the Asian than to the West African element) that it regards itself as here to stay. On the contrary, I would say that there is a great deal of evidence that it regards itself as a caravan which could, and probably will, move on. These are not matters which we can resolve by deduction, it seems to me once again, from Christian principles. They are issues both of fact, which are difficult enough to determine, and of interpretation of fact, and of judgement. My difficulty, confronted by your censure, is to understand—given that I, with the best of my understanding, have applied my mind to this for over twenty years in my own constituency—how, unless my motives can be identified as evil, I can be censured as a Christian.

HUDDLESTON

There are two points I want to make really. I don't regard this as a secular issue—I regard this as a profoundly religious issue, because it affects man where he is as man, and this is the only view I can take. Like yourself, I am a person who has had experience over many years, mine being in Africa and yours being in England, of human situations. If the Christian faith has got nothing to say to human situations, it is not the faith for me. I am just not interested in a religion which is not concerned with man-where-he-is, and if man-where-he-is is subject to the consequences of racialism in any form, that is to say, if man's dignity on both sides of the colour line is lowered by racialism, then I have got to protest.

POWELL

I agree with every word you said ...

HUDDLESTON

Let me just finish. So I think it isn't fair to say that there are no deductions from Christianity. The Institute of Race Relations has carried out an enormous thorough survey ...

POWELL

Which is now three years out of date, and the great part of which I can logically destroy.

HUDDLESTON

Well I would like to see you do it; I am not saying it is impossible to do so but there are certain facts which are conclusive, I would say; and one of those facts is that a very large proportion of those who have come into the country in the last ten or fifteen years are part of this country, that their increase is going to be within this

country. I know West Indian families who regard themselves as wholly and absolutely English; the children will
support, so to speak, the English test team against the
West Indian one, because they are so English.

POWELL

But you see, Bishop, we are merely opposing secular
observations to one another, and then, when you are gratified
with the conclusions that you arrive at, you dignify them
as the consequences of Christian belief. This is what you
are doing. We differ upon facts, upon deductions, and upon
estimates of the future. What I cannot understand (though
I am willing to do so if possible) is why your deductions
are specifically Christian and mine are not.

HUDDLESTON

Simply because my deductions flow from the Christian
Gospel, I would maintain, and you have got to prove that
they don't.

POWELL

But the Christian Gospel tells you nothing either about the
position in the United Kingdom today, or about the prospects
of the position in the United Kingdom twenty years hence,
or about the manner in which people are likely to act in
those circumstances twenty years or so ahead.

HUDDLESTON

No, the Christian Gospel tells me a great deal about man-
where-he-is; whether it's the United Kingdom, or the United
States, or the Republic of Tanzania is totally immaterial.
And if man-where-he-is is concerned, the Christian Gospel is
concerned. How do you interpret such parables as the
parable of the Good Samaritan? What is this telling us
about man?

POWELL

I'll take the dilemma which the parable of the Good
Samaritan presents us with. The lawyer asked, 'who is my
neighbour?' and he was given as answer, 'your neighbour
is everyone, the whole of the world'. I cannot apply this

'neighbour' as a politician. That is to say, those for whom
I am responsible are not the whole of the world. So I am
confronted with a religion which, as it seems to me deliberately and by its very essence, denies certain profound
characteristics of actual human life.

HUDDLESTON
This is the gulf between us, this is the total gulf between us.
You have said that the parable of the Good Samaritan
simply tells us our neighbour is everyone. It certainly tells
us that, but it specifically says: the Samaritan, the enemy
of the Jewish people at that stage of their history, the man
who could not be thought of as a neighbour because of his
religious and cultural differences, this is the man who is to
show love to the other; this is the man, in this particular
historical situation.[3] Now has this not got anything to say to
you about the attitude of the white race to the black race
in its local situation?

POWELL
It says to me that in Christianity there is neither black nor
white, bond nor free; but in the world in which I live there
is black and white, bond and free; there are nations, who
lift up their hands against other nations; and I cannot as
a politician assume that what will happen when the Kingdom comes, is happening or has happened. If I do that,

---

[3] The Bishop and I were both caught by the textual pitfalls of Luke
10.33. The parable has nothing to do with the question and answer about
'the great commandment', to which it has been appended in Luke only.
The attempt to link it by the concluding words: 'Which of these three
was neighbour unto him that fell among thieves? And he said, he that
showed mercy on him' (vv. 36, 37), only reveals this the more starkly.
The question is absurd, and the answer wrong. If the parable had
belonged to the context, the question should have been: 'Which of
these three understood who his neighbour was and acted accordingly?'
The parable itself is an allusion to 2 Chron. 28.15: 'The men took the
captives and with the spoil clothed all that were naked (*stripped him of
his raiment*) among them, and shod them, and gave them to eat and to
drink and anointed them (*pouring in oil and wine*) and carried all the
feeble of them upon asses (*set him on his own beast*), and brought them
to Jericho (*went down from Jerusalem to Jericho*) to their brethren;
then they returned to Samaria'. If the parable has a 'moral', it is that
Jews and Samaritans should remember that they are not merely neighbours (literally) but kinsmen.

then I shall inflict harm upon those for whom I am most responsible.

HUDDLESTON
What then does your Christian faith mean, in terms of everyday living, if it has nothing to say to you about these situations at all, but is only concerned with the Kingdom which is to come?

POWELL
What I have been trying to say throughout, Bishop, is that I find it insuperably difficult to draw deductions from my Christian religion as to the choices which lie open to me in my political life. I can draw deductions as to what should be my frame of mind. I know—not always, but often enough —when I, in my attitude of mind, offend against what is my Christian duty; that I know. But I cannot find enlightenment or guidance as between two alternative policies and courses of action.

HUDDLESTON
Well, supposing the result of a racist speech is to make hundreds, perhaps millions, of Christians in the new African and Asian countries lose their faith in the integrity of the Christian Gospel, is that not our concern?

POWELL
You pose a situation. But then, the assumption is (unless we are questioning motives, which we have agreed not to do) that that speech, the impact of it, and the proposals which it contained, were believed to be necessary to avert a probable or foreseeable evil. Once one has granted that, then we're back again, as I said before, with a choice of disadvantages, and I, with specific responsibilities as a politician, cannot be in doubt where my duty—not my Christian duty, but my duty in my function in society— must lie.

HUDDLESTON
But your Christian duty ought to be the same as your duty in society. This is what I cannot understand with

regard to your attitude. I simply cannot know how you can
separate the two if you are a Christian.

POWELL

I can see that a Christian can have duties in society, but
many of these duties (as, for example, many of my duties
as a politician) don't seem to me to be derivable from the
essential teachings of Christianity, which seem to me,
characteristically and essentially, both to be absolutes and
to be in deliberate and direct conflict with human reality
and human experience.

HUDDLESTON

I agree, there is plenty of conflict between the Christian
faith and the social order in which the Christian Church
operates.

POWELL

It seems to me it must be absolute conflict.

HUDDLESTON

No, I would disagree with that totally. There is a great area
of conflict, there is a great area within the whole Christian
ambit in which men can disagree; but there is one fundamental principle on which the whole of our faith rests, and
that, as I said at the beginning, is the fact—not the idea,
but the fact—that God became man, took flesh, and therefore gave to man-where-he-is a dignity which can not be
taken from him. It is when this dignity is imperilled, that
the Church must speak and act.

POWELL

I can't dissent from what you have just said; but it seems to
me (and this I think is my last word) that what we have
been doing, Bishop, is analysing our respective functions in
society. These functions overlap: you cannot be all priest,
you are bound to be citizen and politician as well; I cannot
be all politician, I have (presumably) to be Christian and
many other things as well. But the emphasis of our respective
functions and purpose in society seems to me distinct. I
feel it is that distinction, which is so easy for either of us to

overlook, which we have been analysing.

III
Meats Offered to Idols
(*Acts 15.29*)

I have before me a news picture, published a year or two ago in a local paper which shows the then Rector of Wolverhampton (now Bishop of Shrewsbury), at a celebration of the Hindu Durga Puja in the town, which was attended by Hindus from all over the Midlands. The accompanying text informs us that an idol of Durga of great sanctity had been flown from Calcutta specially for the festival.

The predicament of the rector in that temple-room in Wolverhampton typifies from one aspect the predicament of the Church as a whole in England today. That predicament has in no wise been created by the presence in England of large and increasing populations of Muslims and pagans. Their presence has only served to sharpen its outlines.

The Church is by nature and of necessity missionary, because it asserts its gospel both to be unique and indispensable and also to be addressed and available to all mankind. It does not, for instance, like Judaism, claim unique truth but address a particular race. It is not, like Hinduism, tolerant of all beliefs and none, but limited to the population of a certain sub-continent. Consequently those who said the Creed and received the sacraments in English towns and villages were told, and accepted, that they were obliged, so far as in them lay, to support and further the preaching of the Gospel and the extension of the Church in 'heathen lands afar'.

The first searching challenge did not, as it happened, originate 'afar'. It arose when a substantial, and presently a large, part of the population of England itself ceased to belong (other than nominally, if that) to any body professing the Christian faith. The question then was: 'With what conviction can we send missions to the heathen afar, when the heathen are here at home, our own kith and kin, in our own land? The mission field, surely, has come home?' Still, there was a tolerable answer to this objection. 'Here in England', it could be said, 'the Church's ministry is offered to all who do not consciously reject it: its witness is interwoven with the physical fabric of our places of habitation and with the social fabric of our institutions, from the church school in the village to the coronation of the sovereign. The fact that there is, as there always has been, an unending task of conversion here in nominally Christian England does not invalidate the duty of conversion overseas'.

Then a day came when the aspect of the 'heathen lands afar' themselves altered radically. The great masses of humanity, in India, in China, and in Africa, which had appeared to offer the vast opportunity and the compelling duty, were now self-consciously nationalist and anti-European. Existing Christian churches, like those of earlier proselytizing religions, particularly Islam, might be more or less accepted as a part of the make-up of the indigenous society; but western proselytizing was shunned or forbidden or at most tolerated only if it wore the garb of medical care or secular instruction. Nationalism and the end of western government had drawn a line beneath the missionary age. Even martyrdom is out of the question when one cannot get a visa.

At the same time as the mission field was folding up overseas, England was in the early stages of a revolutionary change in the composition of her population, to which there has been no precedent or parallel. The Christian Church, on which Asia and Africa were closing their doors as being the cultural badge of the west, was now confronted in England by the religious and cultural badges of large and growing communities transplanted from the very lands where, if 'thick darkness' brooded when the hymn was written, no less 'thick darkness broodeth yet'. Mosques, temples and gurudwaras not only arose round the churches but actually displaced some of them and took over the buildings. Have the clergy, then, faced with this emergency or opportunity, sallied forth, cross in hand, like new Columbas or Augustines, to bring the light of the Gospel not into a far country but to the mission field which had come to Wolverhampton and Bradford? It was certainly not what was expected of them; and it is certainly not what they did. What was expected—nay, clamorously demanded —was that they should participate in the activities of 'race relations' and 'community relations', and assure the new communities not merely of tolerance but of religious and cultural parity. It was thus that, along with the Mayor and Mayoress of Wolverhampton—who, after all, were there in a secular and civic capacity—the rector found himself that day in the company of the goddess Durga's idol, and not to denounce or to confute, but to 'take part', which was what his invitation had said.

Now consider the spectacle not from the point of view of the Durga-worshippers or the race relations industry, but from the point of view of the Christian laity, whether 'in the pew', or no longer in the pew, or would-be in the pew. 'Here', they say to themselves, 'is my parish priest (it may be), who asserts before me, and joins with his people in asserting, the unique truth and indispensability of the Christian revelation and of the sacraments of the Church. Yet he not only does not dare to make those assertions in the face of those to whom he is in duty bound to make them known, not even when they confront him a street or two away from his own church, but he behaves outside it as if religion, and the Christian religion in particular, were indeed a cultural badge and as if one were as good as another, in the sense that one language or one style of architecture may be said to be as good as another. Good manners, tact and tolerance cannot explain this. They are requisite; but they are not relevant here. The reason, surely, why my parish priest dares not preach to the unconverted and dares not behave out of doors as if he believed what he professes indoors is—that he cannot believe what he professes. And if *he* cannot, how can I?'

The case is not special; it is general. Far away from so-called 'race relations' and the mission field which has come to seek out our consciences in our own towns and homes, the same tormenting spectacle confronts the Christian laity—yes, and the would-be Christian laity. From pulpits throughout the land they hear homilies on trade unions and industrial relations, on housing, on economics and productivity, on politics and trade—all of them subjects in which the clergy as such have no special competence and about which in consequence many of those whom they address understand a great deal more than they do. 'Why?' ask the laity. 'Surely it is to avoid having to talk to us about that which is the sole reason and justification for their calling: the doctrine and sacraments of the Church. It is their escapism.' This more and more fervent desire of the clergy to be heard talking about, and concerning themselves in, the business of the hour—and incidentally, in doing so, to be seen wearing the fashionable clothing of the hour—is the symptom of a flight from their own business. The protestation that Christianity is not an escapist religion betrays the uneasy conscience. Who said that it was?

The Bishop of Carlisle in August (1970) brought to public attention through *The Times* a resolution of a conference in his diocese calling on the Government 'to take the lead to integrate public and private investment so that each will reinforce the other to achieve planned objectives of wealth creation'. A church that is applying itself to 'objectives of wealth creation' is a church in flight from itself and, what is more, in flight from its founder, who did not come to teach, 'the achievement of planned objectives of wealth creation'. If that is what the Church is about, then more expert advice and guidance is obtainable elsewhere—be it said with no disrespect to the financial acumen displayed by the Church Commissioners.

It is the failure on the part of the clergy to realize the effect of what they are doing upon those who would naturally look to them, and desire to look to them, that is staggering. At the Methodist Conference in Manchester in July (1970), the Revd. William Gowland, principal of Luton Industrial College, said: 'It is as important for a Christian who holds a trade union card to be at his branch meeting as it is for him to be at Holy Communion'. Incredulous, I approached him for confirmation, imagining that there must somewhere be a misquotation. Promptly and most kindly, and evidently without the least sense that there was anything amiss, Mr Gowland confirmed that that was indeed what he had said, because he was, 'concerned at the absence of Christians and other responsible people from the areas of power and influence within our nation'.

How do the clergy not see what these things convey? Even on an extreme Protestant view of the Holy Communion, to say that the performance of this solemn command of Christ and participation in the central act of the Church throughout its existence is no more important than attendance at a union branch meeting is to reduce Christianity and the Church to a nullity.[1] How comes a Christian minister to tell his flock, in the name of their faith, to get into 'the areas of power and influence within our nation'? 'Power and influence within the nation'—objects as irrelevant, if not abhorrent, to the mission of Christ as 'the creation of wealth': Caesar and Mammon. Significantly it is not even, 'the absence of Christians' from Caesar's throne and hierarchy which causes concern, but 'the absence of Christians *and other responsible people*'. In other words, it is not Christianity which is wanted, but 'responsibility', and the relevance of Christianity is seen as one of several possible bases for 'responsibility' in a secular context.

This once more is escapism, a flight from the only specific function of the clergy and the Church. There may be a

---

[1] I am not sure it is a kindness to record Mr Gowland's comment in his 'Reply to J. Enoch Powell' (*Frontier*, February 1971): 'I find it surprising that Mr Powell, who is generally so careful with the English language, alters the meaning of the words. Far from saying that, "it is *no more* important to attend Holy Communion than a trade union branch meeting", I said that it is *as important* to attend a trade union branch meeting as it is to be at Holy Communion. There is a nuance of difference between the two phrases'. The phrases are indeed different; but if A equals B, B is not greater than A.

number of reasons for regretting it if a Prime Minister or a General Secretary of the TUC is not a Christian; but for the Church there is only one reason, the same, no more and no less, as for regretting that a shop assistant or a garbage collector is not a Christian—namely, that thereby he is a soul lost. Its business is not to find Christians and exhort them to go into politics or trade unionism. Its business is to take the means of salvation to the individuals in 'the areas of power and influence within our nation', no less and no more than to other individuals. This is what St Paul did, to governor and to slave alike, and we know the substance of what he had to say. If people will not listen to the Church when it preaches the Gospel and offers the sacraments, they will certainly not go to it for advice on the business of Caesar or of Mammon.

More and more the Church—and not, so far as I see, only in England—has tried to be heard by saying and doing anything and everything but what it alone can say and do. Not surprisingly, it is heard less and less. Is it too late for it to be itself again?

12

WHAT SHALL WE DO?[1]

When the rector invited my fellow-speakers and myself to come here in Lent, he suggested that we should have 'John the Baptist and the third chapter of St Luke in mind' and indicate 'on what we considered there was a moral need for people to change their minds'. Now, 'change of mind' is the root meaning of the Greek word which we translate 'repentance' when John 'announced baptism of repentance for the ablution of sins'. So I understood straightaway why the rector referred me to John the Baptist. But at first I was puzzled by being also referred to the third chapter of Luke. Why Luke? The account of John the Baptist's call to repentance is in all three synoptic gospels, Matthew, Mark and Luke. (In John's gospel, though the Baptist of course plays a prominent opening part, there happens to be no specific mention of 'repentance'.) So why was I to look up Luke specially, rather than Matthew or Mark?

It must, I concluded, be something which only Luke has; and sure enough there are five verses in Luke alone. Here they are: 'The crowds asked him (John the Baptist), What then shall we do? and he answered and said to them, Let him that hath two cloaks give to him that hath none, and let him that hath eatables do likewise'. This is followed by two special questions and answers: 'The taxgatherers came to be baptised and said to him, Teacher, what shall *we* do? And he said to them, Exact no more than is appointed you. The policemen also asked him, and said, And what shall *we* do? And he said to them, You must not harass or frame

[1] St Botolph Without, London, 2 March 1972.

people, nor try to augment your wages with bribes'.

Is this then the moral content of the 'change of mind' which was to be produced, or symbolized, by the immersion in Jordan? If so, how strange that even that moral content is inserted in one version only, but for which there would have been no knowledge of it at all?

Let us be candid enough to admit to ourselves that this is morality at a pretty humdrum level. To refrain from bribery, corruption and extortion is a test which most of us would probably hope to pass with good marks. There is, it is true, the little piece about sharing out food and clothing, and you can make as much, or as little, of that as you please—it was certainly no novelty in rabbinic teaching—but still there remains a startling contrast between the near triviality of the moral precepts and the vast scale of the setting—the announcement, which is John the Baptist's function in the drama, of the imminent coming of one, 'the latchet of whose shoe etc.', who 'will baptize with the Holy Spirit', who 'will thoroughly purge his threshing floor'. All that must surely be about something on a different plane from the decent standards of behaviour which we have a right to expect from the Inland Revenue and the Metropolitan Police.

This bewildering contrast meets us wherever we open the Gospel and begin to read. The events and the assertions are stupendous; but they do not depend upon a moral doctrine or issue into one. In the Old Testament the awe-inspiring revelation of Jehovah on Mount Sinai announced a precise and extensive code of personal and social behaviour. The revelation of the New Testament, of which the Baptist was the herald or, as the first chapter of John tantalizingly affirms, the 'witness' was utterly different from the Old. It is the difference with which the oldest parts of the New Testament, the Pauline epistles, are constantly preoccupied. St Paul never ceases to examine and re-examine what the new revelation had done to the Jewish law. Sometimes it appeared to have fulfilled it, sometimes to have abolished it; but never did it seem to have supplemented it, or reinforced it, or replaced it by another code.

The startling innovation which filled St Paul's mind was already implicit in the mission of John the Baptist; for the Baptist came to *do* something, not to preach sermons or give moral instruction. The something which he came to do, namely, to baptize, was both symbolic and mysterious— in the original meaning of 'mysterious', which refers to initiation. It was also new; it was also simple; and it was also indispensable.

Nevertheless, though the act of the Baptist had all these characteristics, it was seen by the first Christians to have been at an incomparably lower level than that which it preluded. John's baptism was, 'for the remission of sins'. There is another context in which those same words occur, a context in which they are regularly recalled to every practising Christian throughout the world. Like so many key words in the Bible, they defy precise translation. 'Remission', as our English version has it, is unsatisfactory; and so is 'forgiveness', and so would be 'abolition' or 'cancellation', though these perhaps come nearer to the underlying notion. Whatever translation we use, however, it is precisely the same phrase which occurs at the central point of the central rite of the Church. In the Anglican liturgy it runs: 'This is my blood of the New Testament, which is shed for you and for many for the remission of sins'. The act of the Baptist which produced, or was directed to, the removal of sins was immersion in the water of the Jordan. The act of the Messiah which produced, or was directed to, the same effect was the shedding of his own blood. To those who received the baptism of John correspond those who receive, in a more profound and wonderful manner, the blood of Christ. The act of Christ was, like the act of John but in a more profound and wonderful sense, both new, and simple, and indispensable.

The crowd on Jordan's bank, you remember, are represented as saying to John, 'Master, what shall we do?' The same crowd, the disciples and those further out in the throng, often said to Jesus, 'Master, what shall we do?' They did not receive the kind of answer that they hoped or were expecting. They did not receive moral instruction, nor a social gospel, nor a code of behaviour which they could fulfil. Jesus, who loved, and was steeped in, the law of his people, was not averse to commenting on passages in it in the manner of other Rabbis of his time and before and since; but it was not what he came to do. When he did utter imperatives, his hearers looked in vain for specific content: 'Take up thy cross, follow me' (Matt. 16.24)[2]; 'love one another, as I have loved you' (John 15.12). When he pointed the path of life, he clothed his direction in terms of the unthinkable: 'I am the resurrection and the life, and he that believeth in me, though he were dead, yet shall he live' (John 11.25).

The refusal to answer the question, 'what shall we do?' is essential to Christianity. In the face of its doctrines—incarnation, crucifixion, resurrection, redemption, judgement—the question, 'what then shall we do?' is not so much superfluous as uncomprehending. Yet the refusal to answer is almost intolerable to men and women, in the way that looking straight into the light of the sun is intolerable. Right from the beginning people set to work to fill what they mistook for a void or an omission. We have seen how in Luke the narrative of the baptist was supplied with a few handy questions and answers; and the Gospels, as they have reached us, bear traces of the determination to satisfy the natural demand for some good plain rules of conduct. Much more often, however, it is we ourselves who, by dint of refusing to read what the Gospels actually say, have obtained the answers which Jesus refused to give but which we were set upon finding.

I stand here because I was asked to say on what I thought there is 'a moral need for people to change their minds'. Seeing that I spend my life largely in the advocacy of opinions which I believe to be well founded but which are not yet accepted or at least not yet put into practice, there are naturally a good many matters on which I believe there is a need for people to change their minds; and in some, indeed many, of these cases, I would have little difficulty in persuading myself that this need was a 'moral' need,

[2] See note 2, p. 45.

especially as the word 'moral' is fairly vague and comprehensive. On a political platform or in a lecture hall I would be delighted to give some of them an airing. But that is not where I am. You are here, and I am here, in this church because this is Lent, when the Church prepares itself to face once again and, as best it can, to participate in, the acts of crucifixion and resurrection. In that context there is only one 'change of mind' of which I dare speak. But I dare not call it moral.

Indeed, the change of mind I speak of consists precisely in realizing that morality is not what men need, and that they deceive themselves if they think they can discover and fulfil moral precepts and principles which will make them, individually or collectively, happier or in any way better. You may, or you may not, wish to believe in the self-improvability of man; but it not only has nothing to do with Christianity, but Christianity is a standing contradiction and denial of it.

Day by day we are surrounded by the din, and often by the violence, of those who propose to make men better and happier, and who are sure they know how to do it, if only others would have the sense to give them the necessary powers. Believe it or reject it, hate it or love it, the Church stands in the middle of all this and says: 'No, it is not so'. If anyone should stop and listen, as you have done this afternoon, it says: 'Come, I will show you'. And what does it show us? John the Baptist, to whom the people came, and passed through the water of Jordan, and returned to Jerusalem, that their sins might be taken away from them. But this was prologue—in some sense, even allegory—of the event which was to come, when someone else gave himself to be sacrificed, and in virtue of that act could declare that whoever believed would live even though he was dead or, in other words, would never die.

To entertain this idea and to be penetrated with it is the change of mind, repentance, *metanoia*, of which the baptist was not the announcer but the forerunner. It was this that made it possible to say of the Baptist not merely that he was not just another fashionable preacher ('a reed shaken by the wind') or a leading figure of his time ('clothed in soft raiment'), but that he was greater than the greatest that had gone before: 'Among them that are born of women there hath not risen a greater' (Matt. 11.7–11). The change of mind was to recognize that something new in kind had happened. This is not the sort of change of mind which the prophets had declared to their hearers. It is not the sort of change of mind which, in infinitely various forms, is incessantly preached and advocated in the world outside. It is the change of mind which, whether men receive or reject it, the Church is there to announce and to offer. It dare not, upon pain of ceasing to be itself, substitute any other doctrine.

13

NO MERIT ABOUT IT

A clergyman of my acquaintance, a most excellent clergy-man, recently sent me his parish letter for Lent. I was struck by one sentence in it, all the more because the writer happens to be an outspoken opponent of the uncritical enlistment of Christianity in the cause of trendy fashions—'aid', 'race', 'concern', 'pollution' and the rest. The sentence was this: 'Our Saviour reminds us in the parable of Dives that neglect and indifference towards those that need our help who come within our scope is a dreadful sin deserving rightly God's wrath'. So it is commonly supposed; but so it can only be supposed by either not reading the story—it is, by the way, not a parable—or altering it mentally as we read. Let us take it calmly (Luke 16.19–31).

There was once a rich man who had a splendid time. There was also a destitute person who had a rotten time. When they died the rich man went to hell fire and the beggar went to 'Abraham's bosom', the Jewish heaven.

The first thing to notice is not that the rich man went to hell, but that the beggar went to heaven. There is no sug-gestion whatever that he had done anything to deserve it, or even that he belonged to the ranks of the 'deserving poor'. We are not, for instance, told that he was blind, or crippled, or otherwise unfortunate. So far as we know, he never did a hand's turn in his life or even tried to. Misery, not merit, was his sole passport to paradise.[1]

---

[1] An attempt is sometimes made to extract the moral from the meaning of Lazarus, or Eleazar, viz., 'whom God aids', and to deduce from this that he was a God-trusting beggar, and therefore obtained paradise. Which only shows to what lengths the determination to find an unstated moral somewhere can be pushed. If the 'sores' are intended to be the

Conversely, there is not the slightest suggestion that the rich man did anything wrong.[2] It is we, not the scripture, who blame him for not bringing Lazarus inside and giving him three good meals a day for the rest of his life. If that had been the moral of the story, it would have had to stop with the rich man going to hell, and nothing at all about the destination of Lazarus. As it was, however, Lazarus could count himself exceedingly fortunate to have escaped the attentions of the charitably disposed. If he had been comforted in this world, there would have been no Abraham's bosom for him in the next.

It may be objected: 'But then what is all that about "Moses and the prophets"?' Let us look at it more closely. The rich man's grotesque request in hell that Lazarus should make the incredible journey from heaven, and for no more important or enduring a purpose than to put a drop of water on his tongue, has been rejected with Abraham's assertion that the great gulf between heaven and hell is impassable in either direction; and the story has been rounded off with Abraham's conclusive observation: 'You had your good time, and Lazarus had his bad time, during your lives; now he is comforted and you are tormented'.

Thereupon follows something quite different—another part of the story, or another story—namely, the request that Lazarus be sent from the dead to the rich man's surviving five brothers, in order to 'bear witness' to them and so avoid their finding themselves in hell likewise. If the story had had the supposed moral, the urgent message to get across to the brothers would have been to build or endow a hospital, or at least a rehabilitation centre, with the minimum delay, and that at all costs there must be no repetition of scandals like the Lazarus case.

cause of loss of earning capacity, it is curious that a more obvious disablement was not chosen. The fact is, beggars have sores; and that is all there is to it.

[2] An interpolator, whose work is found in certain late MSS, felt the lack of this so strongly that he inserted the words, 'and no man gave unto him', to imply the refusal of charity; but in fact Lazarus evidently *was* 'fed with the crumbs', as otherwise he would have arrived in Abraham's bosom much sooner. It is a touching Englishism to interpret the behaviour of the dogs as exhibiting a sympathy which men withheld: their attentions were the crowning touch of humiliation.

There is no hint that this was to be the point of the mission; and in fact Abraham retorts in quite general terms: 'They have Moses (i.e. the law) and the prophets, let them hear them'. Lazarus had nothing to add to the law and the prophets. Indeed, there is nothing to indicate that Lazarus bothered his head with the law and the prophets any more than the rich family had evidently done. The point of the dialogue becomes clear only when the rich man persists that his brothers will 'repent' or 'be converted' *if someone comes to them from the dead.* This gives Abraham the opportunity, to which this part of the story has evidently been working up, to reply that those who will not hear the law and the prophets will not 'be persuaded' by a resurrection.

Abraham was to be proved right—and yet only partially right—by the central event of the gospels, the death and resurrection of Christ, which the world apparently ignored. But there was another and more disturbing confirmation. In St John we find the deeply moving narrative of how Jesus actually did bring someone back from the dead (John 11). His name (surely not by chance?) was Lazarus—the only other place where that name appears in the New Testament. This Lazarus, described in the story of his resurrection as the 'friend' of Jesus and brother of Martha and Mary, plays no other part whatsoever in the gospels: he exists only to be raised from the dead. The pithy dictum of Abraham in Luke inspired in John a marvellous piece of imaginative and poetic writing: a man (he might be the Lazarus of the old story) actually did return from the dead, and still no one 'believed'. That passage was John's prelude to Calvary itself.

So the social gospel, warning us not to be indifferent towards those who need our help, has dissolved as we looked at it. In its place have made their appearance two strange, uncomfortable and uncompromising assertions. One tells us that the rich are punished for having been rich, and the wretched rewarded for having been wretched. As Lord Melbourne might have said, 'there is no damned merit about it'. If there is a moral, that is it. The other assertion is that

the impossible happened before our eyes, and it left us all
no different from before—all, or perhaps nearly all, of us.

No wonder people are afraid to read the Bible.

14

DOUBTING THOMAS

We have all heard of 'Doubting Thomas'. The phrase is proverbial for a sceptic. Thomas was the disciple who doubted Our Lord's resurrection. Many no doubt recall the incident which earned for him his unenviable cognomen; but as usual many fewer remember it clearly, or perhaps ever read or listened to it carefully. Significantly, it comes only in the gospel of John, whose author often speaks to us in allegory when he seems to be relating an event (John 20.24–29).

On what we now know as the first Easter Sunday Christ appeared to the disciples. The doors of the room were closed; but Christ suddenly stood in the midst of them, and greeted them, and showed them his hands and side. Thomas, however, was not there; for some reason he was, so to speak, not in church that evening, and when told that his fellow disciples had seen Jesus, he disbelieved them. He did not simply say, however, that, 'unless I too see him, I won't believe it'; he said that he would only believe it if he could put his finger into the holes made by the nails and his hand into the wound made by the spear.

The following Sunday Thomas came to church with the rest. Once again the doors were closed; and once again Christ appeared in the midst of the disciples. He addressed himself to Thomas with the scalding words: 'Reach hither your finger—here are my hands—reach hither your hand and thrust it into my side'. What happened next? Most people, if they were recounting or summarizing the story, would say: 'So then Thomas touched Christ's hands and side, and was convinced'. Many a picture of the incident shows exactly that happening. But that was exactly what did *not* happen. It is the fact that Thomas did *not* touch Christ which is the unspoken high point of the drama. Instead, he exclaimed: 'My lord and my God!'

Thomas had made the physical resurrection of Jesus the test of his believing: 'For me,' said he, 'unlike (apparently) the rest of you, it has to be a body that I can touch and feel and verify as the same body that was crucified'. He was taught a shattering lesson. Suddenly Christ was there, 'the doors being shut'. Those are not wasted words, but a vital element: bodies that can be touched and felt do not pass through closed doors, nor indeed does the Gospel say that Christ did so—only that 'he came and stood'. In this setting the words of Christ to Thomas were not an invitation, 'satisfy yourself, if you must, by touch as well as sight'. They were the opposite. They were a biting irony and they apprised the doubting disciple of something else: not only that the risen Christ whom the disciples had seen was supernatural, but that he had been among them all the time unseen. Else how could he have known what Thomas had said?

The rebuke to Thomas is a rebuke to us: his lesson is ours. Ask not for proof, it says; dream not of a physical resurrection; refuse not the truth of the resurrection because of physical impossibility. As for proof, by reason or the senses, you shall have none. Only, at the utmost reach of faith and understanding, shall you see that by his resurrection he is here, 'in the midst of you'.

INDEX
OF BIBLICAL
REFERENCES

INDEX OF BIBLICAL REFERENCES